Dr. Mack's book will ignite your passion for God's Kingdom in your life and your church. If you are spiritually dry, be prepared for *Passion for Your Kingdom Purpose* to flood your life with His Spirit for life that's on purpose!

Dr. Larry Keefauver

Passion for Your Kingdom Purpose

Sharpen Your Gifts, Test Your Character,
and Move to Your Next Level

PASSION FOR YOUR KINGDOM PURPOSE

*Sharpen Your Gifts, Test Your Character,
and Move to Your Next Level*

by

Dr. Sir Walter L. Mack Jr.

Harrison House
Tulsa, Oklahoma

Cover by Koechel Peterson & Associates, Inc., Minneapolis, Minnesota

12 11 10 09 08   15 14 13 12 11 10 9 8 7 6 5 4

Passion for Your Kingdom Purpose
Sharpen Your Gifts, Test Your Character, and Move to Your Next Level
ISBN 13: 978-1-57794-246-7
ISBN 10: 1-57794-246-9
Copyright © 2004 by Sir Walter Lee Mack, Jr. Ministries
P. O. Box 1919
Clemmons, NC 27012

Published by Harrison House, Inc.
P. O. Box 35035
Tulsa, Oklahoma 74153

DEDICATION

I would like to dedicate this book to my best friend and chief intercessor, my mother, Mrs. Frances Jones Mack, and to my father, the late Dr. Sir Walter Mack Sr., whose life shall always be embedded in my spirit. I thank you for rearing me in a godly home, and for teaching me principles of living humbly before Christ. With all of my love, I dedicate this book to you.

Table of Contents

Foreword xi

Acknowledgments...xiii

Introduction...xv

PART ONE

Kingdom Passion of the Church

Chapter 1	Possessing Passion for Your Life 1
Chapter 2	Understanding the Kingdom of God 9
Chapter 3	Getting to "The Next Level" of Kingdom Passion 15
Chapter 4	Kingdom Passion for True Pentecost 25
Chapter 5	The Priorities of Pentecost 39
Chapter 6	The Power of Pentecost 57
Chapter 7	The Kingdom of God Is Radical............71

PART TWO

The Kingdom Passion of a Man

Chapter 8	The Detoxification of a Man..................91
Chapter 9	The Deliverance of a Kingdom Man 113
Chapter 10	The Defined Kingdom Man 129
Chapter 11	The Discerning Kingdom Man 145
Chapter 12	The Decisive Kingdom Man 159

PART THREE

The Kingdom Passion of a Woman

Chapter 13   The Salvation of a Kingdom Woman 171

Chapter 14   The Security of a Kingdom Woman......177

Chapter 15   The Sociability of a
              Kingdom Woman...............................189

Chapter 16   The Serenity of a Kingdom Woman 209

Chapter 17   The Stamina of a Kingdom Woman 219

Endnotes 229

About the Author...233

FOREWORD

Dr. Sir Walter L. Mack Jr. has tapped into the enormity of passion that is needed by the child of God in order to serve Him. The average believer is constantly seeking God to remove the passions that drive them to sin; not understanding that it is the same passion that drives them to complete God's will.

This book is incredibly insightful to the cognitive approach with biblical directives as to how to allow your passion to work for you. I highly recommend that you read this book. My final words—absolutely ingenious!

—*Bishop Noel Jones*

ACKNOWLEDGMENTS

This assignment has been made possible by the grace of God and the auspices of people who encouraged me by His Spirit.

First, I would like to acknowledge my family for all of the many sacrifices they have made to insure success of my life. To the late Dr. Sir Walter Mack Sr., for being my father and pastor: you taught me the fundamentals of life and ministry. To my mother, Mrs. Frances Jones Mack: for your untiring support and ability to be my mother and my confidant. You are my best friend. To Walteria Spaulding, Cynthia Mack, Monica Mack Covington, and Chris Mack, my siblings, thank you for the years of laughter and fun in the toughest of times. To my brothers-in-law, Clifton C. Spaulding and Mark Covington, thank you for being brothers I know I can lean on. To my sister-in-law, Katina Petty Mack, thank you for your spirit of encouragement. To the joy of my heart, my nephews Mark Covington Jr.: you are a winner; to MaShad Covington: great things are in store for you; to my niece, Melia Covington: you will achieve all that you put your hands to.

Second, I would like to thank my spiritual mentors who are too numerous to name. However, there are a few who have made an indelible print in my life: Dr. Benjamin Alexander Mack, the late C. Eric Lincoln, Dr. Harold A. Carter, Dr. William Augustus Jones, Dr. Charles E. Booth, Dr. William C. Turner, Dr. John Mendez, Dr. Robert C. Scott, Bishop A.L. Jinwright, Pastor Bruce Hurst, and Pastor Curt Cambell. Thank you, Dexter Felder, councilwoman Vivian H. Burke, and entrepreneur Mutter D. Evans for all of your encouragement.

I would be remiss if I did not thank the ministries that allowed me to lead them. I would like to thank the members of Union Baptist Church in Winston-Salem, North Carolina: you are truly a blessing to my life. To my staff: thank you for making me look good. I am thankful that God brought us together. I would also like to thank the New Hope Granville Baptist Church in Oxford, North Carolina: thank you for my first pastoral assignment.

I would like to thank my many friends, cohorts of the gospel, and especially I would like to thank Harrison House, Incorporated, for their kingdom passion and all of their advice in making this book a blessing to many.

Introduction

 W hat is the kingdom of God?

This became a passion for me in my early years of pastoring. After completing my master's of divinity degree, I found myself called to pastor a rural church in Oxford, North Carolina, at the tender age of twenty-six. I had barely crossed the threshold of the church when I found myself in a vicious battle for my new congregation. I truly believe that this horrendous situation came about and continues to happen because many in the body of Christ do not understand or operate in the realm of the kingdom of God.

As a young pastor, I had a passion to see my congregation grow and thrive, but some of the members of my first church questioned my ability to lead a congregation of 350 people. Before I arrived, there had been internal problems that centered on control, leadership responsibilities, and financial accountability, but when I became pastor these problems came to a roaring head.

My intention was to lead the church into a deeper knowledge and understanding of God. I was pleased to find a group of intelligent, zealous, and knowledgeable Christians ready to do whatever it took to grow closer to Him. However, the zeal of the many was threatened when a handful rebelled against me and the order I was trying to establish. These five people desired to control the church. They ignored the voice of the majority, and they were the culprits behind the financial difficulties the church was having. They did not want to do things God's way, according to His Word.

> *Obey them that have the rule over you, and submit yourselves:*
> *for they watch for your souls, as they that must give account,*
> *that they may do it with joy, and not with grief: for that is*
> *unprofitable for you.*
>
> Hebrews 13:17

Whether or not they understood what they were doing, they were violating God's Word in an assignment from hell to destroy the church, and watching over their souls was bringing me a great deal of grief. Meetings were dismissed early due to unruly conduct. Morning worship services were interrupted with confusion. Undercover deputy sheriffs were in attendance on Sundays because vicious threats had been made on my life. Families were divided and lifelong friends were at odds with one another. Most grievous was that unbelievers in the community were told not to come to our church because staying in their lifestyle of sin was much better than being in a church where the people claimed to be saved but acted like they didn't know the Lord. What an indictment against the kingdom of God!

To add insult to injury, these five rebels took the entire church to court for a secular judge to rule over our differences, another gross violation of the Word of God and the kingdom of God.

> *Dare any of you, having a matter against another, go to law before the unjust, and not before the saints?*
>
> *I speak to your shame. Is it so, that there is not a wise man among you? no, not one that shall be able to judge between his brethren?*
>
> *But brother goeth to law with brother, and that before the unbelievers.*
>
> 1 Corinthians 6:1,5-6

On June 4, 1994, the church went to court. Senior citizens, young adults, and children met their deacons, other officers, and me at the courthouse for the proceedings. Arriving with dark sunglasses on my face, I immediately rallied the three hundred faithful in prayer. We prayed that God would fight our battle, that justice would prevail, and that God would move upon the hearts of those who were responsible for our being in this predicament.

The Holy Ghost fell in the hallway of that courthouse, but when I looked up, what I saw was still devastating. Old men and women with canes were crying, some of the members were huffing in anger because they were in this embarrassing situation, and little children were asking their parents what was about to happen. I mustered all the faith and courage I had to enter the courtroom.

The judge heard the case that the five members presented. They requested that he place a restraining order on the new pastor and that all church records be placed in their hands. After their attorney presented their position, God began to work on behalf of the church. While the adversaries intended to destroy the reputation of the pastor and the church, God moved on the heart of the judge. He informed the entire court room of his respect and honor for God's house and not only ruled in our favor, but he also commissioned the five members to leave and start another church if they could not abide by the order that had been established by the majority and their young pastor. I never even had to take the witness stand. We were overjoyed!

After that ruling the church began to flourish. The membership tripled, numerous ministries were birthed, and lost souls were saved. The church is standing strong today, and I was there for six beautiful years before the Lord led me to pastor the Union Baptist Church in Winston-Salem, North Carolina. But in the baptism of fire while pastoring my first church, I began my quest to understand and operate in the realm of the kingdom of God.

It is my hope and prayer that as you read this book, you will be fired with passion for the kingdom of God as I have been over the years. We must have a passion for God's kingdom if we want to avoid the kind of disaster and public humiliation that we experienced in my first church and that many other churches, big and small, are experiencing today. Only a passion for God's kingdom will inspire and prod us to really live God's Word individually and as a body, to throw off our petty differences and denominational barriers, and to allow Jesus to truly be the head of all believers.

Kingdom passion is the only motivation the Church can have if she wants to be the glorious bride of Christ, defeat hell's gates, and establish the covenant of God in the earth. Do you have passion for God's kingdom? If you don't know, read and find out. If you don't have passion or you don't have enough passion, read on and get fired up. And if you already have passion for God's kingdom, read on and soar to new heights!

Part One

~

KINGDOM PASSION
OF THE CHURCH

1

POSSESSING PASSION
FOR YOUR LIFE

*P*assion is like a mighty current that causes a river to flow into the ocean or the rushing wind that drives the clouds across the sky. Passion moves. Passion produces. Passion brings forth fruit. Passion is the soul becoming one with purpose, the heart and mind becoming transformed by the revelation of God's Word and will. Passion empowers believers to bring forth the destiny God ordained for them. And the kingdom of God can only manifest through the passion of born-again, Spirit-filled believers.

Passion is ignited by revelation of God and His kingdom. When we seek first the kingdom of God, we desire God's mind and heart for our lives. As He reveals His heart and mind for our lives, passion for Him and His kingdom begins to blaze inside us. When He reveals the works and responsibilities He has assigned us, we must keep our passion for God's kingdom in order to fulfill our divine destiny. Our passion for the kingdom is fueled by our passion for what God has called us to be and do. Likewise, our passion for what God has called us to be and do fuels our passion for the kingdom. Therefore, it is essential for us to know our position and function in God's kingdom—passionately.

Here Am I, Send Me

When we consider the work and responsibility that is involved in the enhancement and the development of the kingdom, we cannot negate the necessity for human involvement and responsibility. This involves the spreading of Jesus' message that the kingdom of God has come, that it is with us and among us, and that we must be born again to enter and see it. In many cases human involvement and responsibility go without challenge because too often we do not understand our image, purpose, direction, or destiny. It is in the image of God, in the *imago dei,* that God created us (see Gen. 1:26). The image is the very characteristic of God's nature. In Genesis 1:26, the Hebrew word translated "image" is the Hebrew word *tselem.*[1] However, in the New Testament, "image" comes from the Greek word *eikon,* which means the character of God.[2] It appears that God's original design for humanity was for our image to be a partaker of His divine character and nature. While there are many characteristics that are ascribed to the very nature of God, such as, holiness, sovereignty, and omnipotence, there is no characteristic that stands out more profoundly for me than the characteristic of a God who is always on some assignment. If it is difficult for you to imagine God on an assignment, see God passionately on an assignment through Jesus Christ.

The passion assignment of Christ is so real and relevant that in many instances of the New Testament, we see a Christ who is determined about accomplishing what others perceive as trivial. In John 4:34 He reveals to the disciples His assignment, which is twofold: 1) to do the will of God who sent Him, and 2) to finish the work. For example, before Jesus meets the woman at the well, John 4:4 states, "And he must needs go through Samaria." The key word is "need." It declares that Jesus didn't just happen to go through Samaria because he wanted to but because he needed to. He didn't just go through Samaria because He thought it was a pretty place to see or because He lacked other ways to get to where he was going. The Holy Spirit was firmly directing His path. The need became very clear when He met the woman at the well. She needed Jesus to minister to her and save her. Then she received the same passion that compelled Jesus to go to Samaria, and God used her to preach the gospel to her entire city.

Another instance of need is when the time came for Jesus to offer Himself as a sacrifice. The week of His crucifixion, also known as Passion or Holy Week, began on Palm Sunday with Jesus riding triumphantly into Jerusalem on an ass.

And when they came nigh to Jerusalem, unto Bethphage and Bethany, at the mount of Olives, he sendeth forth two of his disciples,

And saith unto them, Go your way into the village over against you: and as soon as ye be entered into it, ye shall find a colt tied, whereon never man sat; loose him, and bring him.

3

And if any man say unto you, Why do ye this? say ye that the
Lord hath need of him; *and straightway he will send him hither.*

Mark 11:1-3 (italics mine)

Why did Jesus need to ride into Jerusalem on an ass? He had
come to fulfill the messianic prophecies like this one in the book
of Zechariah.

Rejoice greatly, O daughter of Zion; shout, O daughter of
Jerusalem: behold, thy King cometh unto thee: he is just, and
having salvation; lowly, and riding upon an ass, and upon a
colt the foal of an ass.

Zechariah 9:9 (italics mine)

This prophetic verse of Scripture explicitly declares that the
Messiah will ride into Jerusalem on an ass, not a camel and not
on the shoulders of others. Jesus needed an ass to do the will of
His Father and fulfill prophecy. This appeared to be a small,
trivial matter to those not familiar with the messianic prophecies, but it was a vital necessity to Jesus.

Kingdom assignment begins with a need. While in many
instances we do not like to see God being in need of anything,
the truth of the matter is that He needs us to do His will just as
He needed Jesus to do His will. God has need of us. I think this
is illustrated profoundly in Isaiah, the 6th chapter, when God
sanctified the tongue of Isaiah.

Also I heard the voice of the Lord, saying, Whom shall I send,
and who will go for us? Then said I, Here am I; send me.

Isaiah 6:8

Clearly there is a task that God needs done, and Isaiah volunteers to do it. And the reference to "us" is in reference to God and Isaiah. It is simply an expression of a desire that both God and Isaiah had. We know that Isaiah had the same desire as God because no conversion ever happens without one taking on the desires of God. Perhaps this is why Isaiah says in Isaiah 48:16, "Come ye near unto me, hear ye this; I have not spoken in secret from the beginning; from the time that it was, there am I; and I the Lord God and His Spirit have sent me." Though God had the desire, He needed somebody to go for Him, so Isaiah said, "Here am I; send me."

Picture a husband and wife reading in bed, and one says to the other, "Honey, I have a taste for some cold ice cream." The other says, "Honey, I do as well." Then they both look at each other and say, "Who's going to get it?" After a brief debate, one gives in and says, "I'll go." In other words, "Here am I; send me." Like God and Isaiah, both have a desire but only one goes to fulfill it.

Developing passion for your kingdom assignment begins with these two concepts: a "need" and "Here am I; send me." So many times we think that our assignment has to be at a lofty level of preaching, teaching, and working miracles. But our assignment begins when we detect a need in our family, church, community, the company where we work, the school we attend, or a relationship we have. We are often distracted by the grander things of life and overlook the small areas of need that are our kingdom assignment for that moment. Our kingdom assignment is simply discovering what is needed right where we are.

In Ephesians 1:18-19, Paul the apostle prayed for the church in Ephesus to know the hope of their calling or vocation. P.T. Forsyth says that "Christianity is the perfect religion...not the perfect religion in the sense of being revealed as finished, rounded, or symmetrical...but it holds up a perfect ideal that every one is called and each one is called to it (Christianity). It is a religion that issues from the perfect One, and returns to His perfection."[3]

Passion for the Need?—You've Heard the Call!

The need that God gives you passion for is the explicit assignment that He is calling you to fulfill. What drives you, gets your adrenaline going, and brings excitement to your life is probably your kingdom assignment. For example, one of my senior members who retired as a van driver for an airport shuttle service came to me and said, "Pastor, I love to drive, and I have been driving for the airport for years. Now I'm retired and I want to drive for the church." Then he said, "I want to use my time driving senior members to the drug store, grocery store, to pay bills, anywhere they want to go except the shopping mall, because pastor, me and the mall just don't get along." He started that ministry, and he loves it and the senior members do too. The need that gets your blood flowing with excitement indicates what your assignment is.

Whether your assignment is something others are already doing or something of unique design, it is your assignment. It is the need you have been called by God to fill. It is time for you to possess and take proper ownership of the vocation and call that God has deposited in your spirit to do. There is always a senior citizen in the community or in your church who needs a ride somewhere. There is always a child who needs a mentor, and your kingdom assignment may be to guide, motivate, and help them with issues such as self-esteem, goal setting, school-work, and peer pressure. Your church may need you in the choir, as an usher, or as a Sunday school teacher. As a pastor, I can tell you that churches always need another van driver, another nursery worker, or another volunteer in the soup kitchen or in the prison ministry. Many great missionaries began in soup kitchens and many great preachers learn God's compassion for people in prison ministry.

Finding kingdom assignments by discovering needs was put into practice in our church recently. I did a teaching series on "Networking Resources for the Kingdom," and our members saw a need for utilizing the gifts and talents available in our congregation. A committee was organized to develop a membership resource manual that listed the gifts and talents of each member, from sewing clothes to repairing cars. Now, when a member needs to have something done, they consider another member in the church who has identified themselves as having this gift or talent or skill. More importantly, members found a way to connect their professions, hobbies, or areas of expertise with the kingdom.

Again, kingdom assignments are not at angelic levels and lofty heights but right where you are. Learn to discover a need and use what you have. Be a passionate, yielded vessel who says, "Here am I, Lord; send me." Here is my challenge to you today.

- Identify at least three gifts or talents you operate in with ease and keen understanding.

- What can you do in your home, community, or church to use your gifts or talents?

- Seek an organization or auxiliary in your community that is doing the work that you have identified as your assignment. Network with or join that group and get the kingdom assignment done.

2

UNDERSTANDING THE KINGDOM OF GOD

The clearest definition the Bible gives of the kingdom of God is in Romans 14:17: "For the kingdom of God is not meat and drink; but righteousness, and peace, and joy in the Holy Ghost." We learn more about the nature of the kingdom of God from the many references in both the Old and New Testaments. Jesus taught, "The kingdom of God is like . . ." and then told parables to illustrate. In Mark 4:11 He says, "Unto you it is given to know the mystery of the kingdom of God." He refers to the kingdom as a mystery, but indicates that it shall be revealed to those who believe.

Jesus states emphatically to Nicodemus in John 3 that in order to see and enter the kingdom of God, we must be born again. Thus, if we have been born again, we should be able to see and know that we abide in the kingdom of God.

Jesus answered and said unto him, Verily, verily, I say unto thee, Except a man be born again, he cannot see the kingdom of God.

Jesus answered, Verily, verily, I say unto thee, Except a man be born of water and of the Spirit, he cannot enter into the kingdom of God.

That which is born of the flesh is flesh; and that which is born of the Spirit is spirit.

Marvel not that I said unto thee, Ye must be born again.

The wind bloweth where it listeth, and thou hearest the sound thereof, but canst not tell whence it cometh, and whither it goeth: so is every one that is born of the Spirit.

John 3:3,5-8

In this passage of Scripture, Jesus also reveals that the kingdom of God is a spiritual kingdom and not a natural, tangible one. Just before He was crucified, in John 18:26, He told Pontius Pilate that His kingdom was not of this world. So we know that the mystery of God's kingdom will be revealed to us in the Spirit.

God is a Spirit: and they that worship him must worship him in spirit and in truth.

John 4:24

The kingdom of God is a mystery unless you are born of the Spirit. This kingdom is spiritually known and spiritually understood because God Himself is a spirit being. I believe that as we consider the dimension in which God exists and how He is defined, we will then have a deeper understanding of what God intends to accomplish in His kingdom and how we fit into His intentions.

*For my thoughts are not your thoughts, neither are your ways
my ways, saith the Lord.*

*For as the heavens are higher than the earth, so are my ways
higher than your ways, and my thoughts than your thoughts.*

Isaiah 55:8-9

God is a spirit being who thinks. Throughout God's Word, there is a recurring theme that the kingdom of God is established on earth as God's thoughts become our thoughts. From Genesis to Revelation, we see that everything that exists began with a thought. God thought and then spoke what He thought. In Genesis 1 He thought *Let there be light* and then He said, "Let there be light."

*For as the rain cometh down, and the snow from heaven, and
returneth not thither, but watereth the earth, and maketh it
bring forth and bud, that it may give seed to the sower, and
bread to the eater:*

*So shall my word be that goeth forth out of my mouth: it shall
not return unto me void, but it shall accomplish that which I
please, and it shall prosper in the thing whereto I sent it.*

Isaiah 55:10,11

In the same passage that God tells us His thoughts are not like our thoughts, He says that His spoken words always accomplish His will and prosper in His purposes. God equates His thoughts with His Word. The Bible tells us that God made everything by His Word and that Jesus was the embodiment of His Word.

*In the beginning was the Word, and the Word was with God,
and the Word was God.*

11

The same was in the beginning with God.

All things were made by him; and without him was not any thing made that was made.

And the Word was made flesh, and dwelt among us, (and we beheld his glory, the glory as of the only begotten of the Father,) full of grace and truth.

John 1:1-3,14

In the Greek language, "Word" is *logos. Logos* refers to the expression of thought.[1] Jesus Christ is the physical revelation in this earth of the thoughts of God. Therefore, Jesus, the living Word of God, is also the manifestation of the kingdom of God. The New Testament also translates the Greek word *rhema* as "Word." As God's written or spoken Word,[2] *rhema* also reveals God's kingdom to us. Both of these Greek words give us clear indication that the Word of God—whether written or spoken—reveals the kingdom of God.

We understand that much can be extracted about God's thoughts through the life of Jesus Christ, who is the *logos,* the Living Word. But we can also discover God's thoughts through His written Word, the Old and New Testaments. The Word of God is our authority to know the mysteries of the kingdom of God. Whatever is established in Jesus Christ and the Word of God is what we should desire for our lives, our families, our ministries, and our communities.

In simple terms, the Church establishes the kingdom of God on this earth as they abide in God's Word in their lives, individually and collectively. What happened in my first church is happening in churches all over the world because they have lost focus on what the kingdom of God is all about. The kingdom of God manifests in our lives when God's thoughts and ways become our thoughts and ways, when His Word rules our hearts and minds and actions.

The kingdom of God is not limited by physical territory because it is a spiritual kingdom. It is a manifestation of God's Spirit and truth in every capacity of human endeavor. The kingdom of God is established when God's perspective impacts individuals, groups, and thus situations. It is essential for those who are born again to have God's perspective for every area of their lives. Only then can they have clarity on what they are to do and be in God's kingdom, and this is not a one-time event or something that occurs from time to time. Maintaining God's perspective is living by the Word and the Spirit on a daily basis. When individuals and churches forget this, they fall or fail.

So many began their missions with a kingdom agenda, "Let God's Word and Spirit have total rule and authority." Then over time, they forgot to remind themselves of this truth and hold themselves accountable for it. Subtly and slowly, they became engrossed with busy activities and mundane matters that had very little to do with their missions. Their kingdom agenda evolved into another agenda that was not fired and formed by the Word and the Spirit, allowing frivolous activity to dominate and give a false sense of fulfillment.

Consequently, the kingdom is inhabited by conditioned saints who just barely make it through another church meeting, despondently attending some auxiliary gathering or church program, and coming to worship because it is the traditional, obligatory thing to do. What an insult to God!

The kingdom of God is the government of God that rules our earthly affairs. It is not an appendage to or a secondary voice in our earthly affairs. The kingdom supercedes and dictates our church and ministry activities, but when our attitude is prompted by obligation instead of passion, our concept of the kingdom is reduced to a legal and moral binding ritual.

In its most authentic form, the kingdom of God impacts the world with God's ways, thoughts, and actions. Kingdom concepts are universal and transcend cultures, people groups, and denominations. Therefore, the purpose of the kingdom of God is to reveal the move of the Holy Spirit in every situation, making certain that His Word and will are performed, and God is glorified in the process.

Jesus eloquently prayed, "Thy kingdom come, thy will be done, on earth as it is in heaven" (Matt. 6:10). Isn't it interesting that He used the words "kingdom" and "will" in the same thought? The kingdom is God's will—not our will—being done on earth. Thus, it is what God desires to bring from the spiritual realm to the physical realm. It is God implanting Himself in us for a greater cause and responsibility so that heaven manifests on earth. When the Church has a passion for the kingdom of God by thinking, speaking, and acting according to the Word and the Spirit, God can restore His divine pattern to the earth.

3

GETTING TO "THE NEXT LEVEL" OF KINGDOM PASSION

*O*ne of the most popular phrases dominating Christian airwaves, church services, and conferences is this term "the next level." Worship services that move in the liberty and emancipation of the Holy Spirit often use this term to describe deliverance that takes a believer from one level of freedom in the Spirit to the next. But how do we capture the next level of kingdom passion? What does the next level look like? What does it feel like? Where can I find it? And just how does God move His people to higher revelations and modes of living?

Recently one of my members grabbed me after a worship service and said, "Pastor, it's time for us to move to the next level." Well, of course this messed my spirit up because we had just experienced a time of worship when the anointing had flowed freely, the choir sang angelically, the Word went forth powerfully, deliverance broke out at the altar, and I thought we had gone to the next level. At least I was at another level!

That's when I realized that we use the term "the next level" all the time and have never actually defined what it means. Obviously, what the next level meant to me was not at all what it meant to that member of my church. It was then that I realized that the next level for one might not be the next level for another.

If we did a spiritual autopsy of this particular situation, I must submit that the next level is not necessarily more shouting, tongue speaking, prophesying, or preaching and teaching. While all of these components are important functions in the body of Christ, to operate in these specific areas does not necessarily suggest that your church or your ministry is at the next level. So then, what is the next level?

Letting the Holy Spirit Lead

The next level is simply ascribing to the operation of the Holy Spirit. It is when we allow the Holy Spirit to operate in us and through us that we undisputedly move into another realm of worship, praise, holiness, understanding, and Christian witness. That is the next level of kingdom passion! And it can vary from person to person and church to church.

Every one does not interpret the move of the Spirit in the same fashion, so the Spirit may move differently from each individual perspective. In other words, one believer may go to the next level by prophesying or speaking in other tongues. Another may be so touched in their heart that they just rock from side to side with tears rolling down their cheeks. Another may simply begin to read their Bible for three hours straight, seeking greater revelation of God's Word for their life. Someone else may sit and hear the testimonies of the saints and get to their next level. But each one is stoking the fire of kingdom passion within them.

Regardless of how the Holy Spirit manifests at any given moment, what I believe is congruent in these scenarios is that the Holy Spirit is in charge, and He takes each individual and thus the corporate body to the next level. When we allow the Holy Spirit to be in charge, our lives are elevated to unimaginable heights or taken into an abyss of spiritual renewal and heightened awareness of God's sovereignty and power in our lives.

When the Holy Spirit is in charge in church, He brings us together and takes us to the next level together. Our concern is not what people are wearing, where we're going to eat after service, or that Brother Jones has fallen asleep during the pastor's sermon again. Instead, in the Spirit there is an encounter with the divine that makes humanity take a back seat and enables God to produce a work in the tabernacles of His people. In the Spirit, one's level of significance is solely determined by God's standard. When God's people are simply under the control of the Holy Spirit, regardless of race, gender, educational achievements, socio-economic status, or position in the church, everybody is then at the same level *because it is His level.*

When we understand that the next level is simply when God's Spirit flows freely within our lives wherever we are and whatever we are doing, then we can also see how this puts the ten-thousand-member church on the same level as the twenty-member church. It would seem that the ten-thousand-member church could produce more resources and thus do things at a higher level of excellence and reach more people. However, resource excellence should not be confused with spiritual excellence. Resource excellence can happen without a church being open for the move of the Spirit. There are churches that have million-dollar budgets, but the atmosphere in them is spiritually foul and uninviting. A twenty-member church may not have tremendous resources, but when you walk into that little storefront building, you feel love, power, joy, peace—and the Holy Spirit is in charge.

In the Spirit, the deacon is no greater than the parking attendant, the missionary is no greater than the nursery worker, and the sound technician is no greater than the choir member. The only leader is the Holy Spirit, who moves us all to the next level of love, unity, and understanding. That is where God can freely use us as individuals and as a body to manifest His kingdom. And *that* is the next level!

The Key of Humility

Spiritual openness, trust, and respect for the direction of God's move are also keys to the next level for God's people. What am I really talking about here? The next level demands the passionate denial of our will in the challenge of doing God's will in every area of human endeavor. We get to the next level of kingdom passion through simple humility—not our will but His will be done.

> *Then cometh Jesus with them unto a place called Gethsemane, and saith unto the disciples, Sit ye here, while I go and pray yonder.*
>
> *And he took with him Peter and the two sons of Zebedee, and began to be sorrowful and very heavy.*
>
> *Then saith he unto them, My soul is exceeding sorrowful, even unto death: tarry ye here, and watch with me.*
>
> *And he went a little farther, and fell on his face, and prayed, saying, O my Father, if it be possible, let this cup pass from me: nevertheless not as I will, but as thou wilt.*
>
> Matthew 26:36-39

True humility was most profoundly expressed in the passion of Jesus as He submitted Himself to the Father's will, which meant He allowed Himself to be crucified by men. Jesus prayed what I call the model prayer in the Garden of Gethsemane. In this particular prayer, He asked that what He was about to face be taken away. In other words, the humanity of Jesus Christ did not want to meet the divinity of Jesus Christ. Jesus began to pray, "Father, if it be possible, let this cup pass from me."

Some time ago the Lord gave me some insight on this passage and I preached a sermon titled, "A Prayer I'm Glad the Lord Didn't Answer." In that sermon I explained that there are some things in our lives we ask God for, and in our minds we really believe that we need those things. But God sees further than we do, and He does not give them to us. Oftentimes we become angry, upset, and discouraged because He doesn't answer our prayer about a relationship, a job, a goal, an idea, or a ministry plan. But in retrospect, we can attest that we didn't understand everything then, and now we are relieved that He didn't bless us with whatever it was we thought we needed!

Aren't you glad God didn't give you that job at the company that laid off workers and closed down exactly one year after you applied? Aren't you glad God didn't answer your prayer for that person to not leave your ministry team because you thought they were faithful but later you discovered otherwise? Some prayers you are glad the Lord doesn't answer. Humility is trusting God beyond your own understanding of what you desire or think you need. It is the "nevertheless" factor.

Jesus prayed, "Nevertheless, not as I will, but as thou wilt." This is going to the next level through humility. I don't know the kind of power that was wrapped up in that word "nevertheless," but whatever power it was, it moved Jesus to say, "not as I will, but as thou wilt." Humbling yourself to the perfect plan and will of God opens the door for God to take you to new kingdom assignments, kingdom horizons, and kingdom purposes.

Whosoever therefore shall humble himself as this little child, the same is greatest in the kingdom of heaven.

Matthew 18:4

Humility not only aligns us with God's perfect plan and will for our lives, but also positions us for blessing and honor. P.T. Forsyth declares, "Humility is a frame of perfect mind not possible except to faith. It is no more depression and poverty of spirit than it is loud self-depreciation. It rests on our deep sense of God's unspeakable gift, on a deep sense of our sin as mastered by God, on a deep sense of the Cross as the power which won that victory....It is the soul's attitude towards God."[1]

I am moved up a level when I humble myself before the Lord. I am taken to new dimensions when I see and acknowledge how great and majestic He is and how astounding it is that He paid such a tremendous price for me to be His son, to enjoy His company, and to share in His exploits. My life is put into proper perspective when I submit all that I have to Him.

We simply cannot walk in our kingdom assignments with passion without being humble before our God. Many believers never obtain all that God has for them or become whole in Him because they do not develop and practice humility. According to the Scriptures, there are two ways to be humbled.

> *And whosoever shall exalt himself shall be abased; and he that shall humble himself shall be exalted.*
>
> Matthew 23:12

Either we can humble ourselves or God will humble us. Obviously, it is far better for us to humble ourselves! We can stay humble before the Lord by continuously reminding ourselves that everything we are and have comes from Him, that everything we do is orchestrated and empowered by Him, and that every blessing we enjoy comes from Him. Our only pride is in what He has done, is doing, and will do in our lives.

Again, considering the two options, I would prefer to humble myself, rather than be in a position where God has to humble me. In this case, the next level is not up! For those who allow arrogance, conceit, and narcissism to control their lives, according to the Bible their next level is down. Those who exalt themselves will be brought low.

God resisteth the proud, and giveth grace to the humble.

Humble yourselves therefore under the mighty hand of God, that he may exalt you in due time.

1 Peter 5:5,6

For Christians, going to the next level of kingdom passion is humbly allowing the Word to rule our hearts and the Spirit to operate freely in our lives. Going to the next level in this way provides the evidence to those around us that the kingdom of God is here.

Staying Open

Humility allows believers, churches, and ministries to stay open to new ways and new ideas of doing ministry. Some concepts and programs may have been good for the past, but today we must question their relevance. Moreover, it is time for the people of God to be open to new revelation and teaching about the Scriptures. We cannot be so arrogant as to think that we understand the Word of God in its totality and that the Holy Spirit has nothing else to reveal.

Humility also allows believers, churches, and ministries to stay open and recognize people who have never been used in ministry as needed ministers in God's kingdom. The Holy Spirit is converting ex-convicts and making them deacons in churches. He is delivering drug pushers and raising them up to be leaders of youth ministries. He is transforming the lives of homosexuals and lesbians and bringing forth their powerful testimonies so that others who are caught in this web of deception and perversion can be set free.

We must always stay open to the move of the Holy Spirit, who takes us to the next level, and then the next level, and the next level of kingdom passion. We maintain our passion for the kingdom by staying open for new moves of God and new shifts in the body of Christ. This does not mean that what has taken place in the past was not of God or did no good for the kingdom, but we must have fresh manna every morning, every season, to keep kingdom passion burning brightly. Here is my challenge to you today.

- Don't quench the Holy Spirit in any area of your life. Let Him have total freedom to move you from one level to the next.

- Be humble. Talk more about what God has done in your life, rather than what you have accomplished for Him.

- Stay open to new ideas, revelation, moves of God, and methods of ministry.

4

KINGDOM PASSION FOR TRUE PENTECOST

*I*t is ironic that the hallmark of Pentecost as described in Acts, chapter 2, is unity. In this historic, supernatural birth of the Church, the Holy Spirit brings a bunch of believers into one accord. Why is this ironic? Today, there is nothing more theologically controversial and divisive than the subject of Pentecost and the relevance and legitimacy of the Pentecostal experience for believers now.

One of the ways the enemy destroys the work and the will of God in our lives, which keeps the kingdom of God from manifesting, is to keep the people of God divided. And when I speak of the people of God, I am referring to the Church universal. The strongest antichrist influence on the body of Christ produces division, bifurcation, and vile malignancy. The enemy knows that if he can keep the Church of Jesus Christ embroiled in controversy and conflict, she will not be able to produce the fruit of righteousness nor walk in the power and authority given to her.

If Satan can keep the Presbyterians fighting the Methodists, the Christian Methodist Episcopals fighting the African Methodist Episcopals, the Disciples of Christ fighting the Church of God in Christ, the Apostolics fighting the Holiness groups, the Conservative Baptists fighting the National and Progressive Baptists, the Full Gospel believers fighting the Evangelicals—then he doesn't have to worry about the kingdom of God manifesting on the earth.

If we are not careful in our denominations, we will repeat what happened in 1906, when a preacher by the name of William J. Seymour started a movement that divided our churches right down the middle. The Pentecostal Movement in the United States is traced back to 1901 in Topeka, Kansas. C.F. Parham, a Methodist minister, and several of his parishioners waited and prayed until they received the baptism of the Holy Spirit and spoke in tongues.[1] Later in 1906, Seymour gathered a group of believers on a street called Azusa in Los Angeles, California. This group met in a shack and began to speak in tongues and move in the gifts of the Spirit, among other things.

Most believers and the denominations of which they were a part did not know what to think about this. As a matter of fact, on April 18, 1906, *The Los Angeles Times* headlined an article on the phenomenon this way, "Weird Babel Happening on Azusa Street." The article went on to say, "There is a new sect of fanatics who are breathing strange utterances, and mouthing a creed which it would seem no sane mortal could understand. Meetings are held in a tumbled down shack, and the night is made hideous in the neighborhood by the howling of worshipers. And from windows of that old building, there could be heard the speaking of tongues, and the sounds of deliverance."

When the word got out that this preacher, William J. Seymour, introduced the Pentecostal Movement in that place, churches across America were divided over that very issue. Those who didn't understand the Pentecostal Movement or who had been taught that all these things had passed away after the first century began to distance themselves from the Pentecostals. They called speaking in tongues, laying on of hands, and being slain in the spirit forms of unintelligence, heresies, and completely unorthodox practices for the Church. Thus, the Pentecostal Movement divided the church in America, and our missionaries carried that division to other countries.

True Worshipers

The Pentecostal Movement changed the traditions and rituals of worship in the church service. In years of ministry, I have discovered that because experiences vary from one to another, no one is really in a position to say what it takes for someone else to make contact with God. We have to be mindful that none of us are in a position to judge the worship and the praise of another because in a moment of worship and praise we don't have time to hear a person's life story. True kingdom worship allows one to convene with God as they need to and according to their understanding.

When Isaiah saw the Lord seated high and exalted (see Isa. 6:3) he said, "the whole earth is full of his glory." In other words, as Isaiah worshiped the Lord he thought the whole earth was doing what he was doing. So it is when real worship and praise happens in a person's life. If you are in a place where all you can see is the glory of the Lord, you are not going to be noticing or caring what someone is wearing, if they have body piercings, or whether or not they are crying, shaking, or shouting. You are not concerned about anything but God. When real worship happens you literally think that the whole earth is full of God's glory. That is why true worshipers maintain kingdom passion.

The division between Pentecostals and non-Pentecostals was intensified when Pentecostals not only decided you were an inferior Christian if you didn't speak in tongues, but that they owned the copyright to tongues. Nobody else could lay hands on a believer to receive the baptism of the Holy Ghost but the Pentecostals. This mentality is dangerous because no one denomination or group has a monopoly on God, and the kingdom of God embraces diversity. We often make God fit into our denominations, when our denominations reflect more of us than they reflect God, His Word, or His Spirit.

Some of us have a wrong kind of passion. This is a passion for our denomination. This passion is arrogant and divisive. It destroys Church unity through animosity and hatred, impairs the kingdom of God, and makes the Church a laughingstock and mockery before the world we are trying to reach. Church fights, church splits, and church confusion can all occur when this deadly kind of passion controls God's people.

A kingdom church and a kingdom Christian allow God's Spirit to move where He chooses, how He chooses, and when He chooses. Pentecostalism has nothing to do with a denomination as much as it does a revelation of God's Word that the believers in the Upper Room obeyed Jesus' command to tarry in Jerusalem and fully—individually and corporately—submitted themselves to the move of the Holy Spirit, which led to a powerful experience in God. Because the Pentecostal experience is simply allowing the Holy Spirit to have His way, you don't have to have the Pentecostal label *outside* your church to have a Pentecostal experience *inside* your church.

The power of Pentecost is not in the inscription on a church marquee but that believers understand that kingdom passion empowers them to maximize their potential and advance God's kingdom in the earth. You can be a Baptist on the outside and have a Pentecostal experience on the inside. Your service program can bear the symbol of the Methodists, Presbyterians, or Episcopalians; and your program can still be interrupted by the Holy Spirit in a Pentecostal experience. Again, Pentecostalism has nothing to do with a denomination, but rather it has to do with an encounter with the Living God.

What Is Pentecost?

In the Old Testament, Pentecost was simply a feast Israel celebrated fifty days after the ceremony of the barley sheaf during

Passover. It was the time when Jews gathered to celebrate the harvest God had produced in the previous season. But after Jesus was crucified at Passover and then was resurrected three days later, something phenomenal happened fifty days later in Jerusalem when Pentecost came.

> *And when the day of Pentecost was fully come, they were all with one accord in one place.*
>
> *And suddenly there came a sound from heaven as of a rushing mighty wind, and it filled all the house where they were sitting.*
>
> *And there appeared unto them cloven tongues like as of fire, and it sat upon each of them.*
>
> *And they were all filled with the Holy Ghost, and began to speak with other tongues, as the Spirit gave them utterance.*
>
> Acts 2:1-4

In the New Testament, Pentecost became the day when the Holy Spirit brought power to the Church. After these saints were baptized in the Holy Spirit, they ran out into the streets literally on fire for God. Jews from every nation were there and heard the gospel preached to them in their own languages. When some mocked and accused the believers of being drunk, Peter, who days before was cowering and afraid to admit he even had met Jesus, stood up and preached one of the most powerful messages in history. (See Acts 2:5-41.)

Pentecost brought more than tongues to the Church. The Holy Ghost marked the Day of Pentecost with holiness, miracles, and revelation. And if that is our biblical definition of Pentecost, then right now we all stand in need of it! Pentecost was the experience that birthed the Church, with its roots established in the work and doctrine of Jesus Christ, into a life of holiness, miracles, and revelation. When we consider the status of the universal Church today, all of us need more of these things in our families, our personal lives, and our churches. Therefore, let's examine and define what we mean by holiness, miracles, and revelation.

Holiness in the New Testament is generally translated from the Greek word *hagiasmos,* which means a form of sanctification or separation unto God[2] and apart from worldly, fleshly, and demonic things. Holiness is a lifestyle that glorifies God and sets one apart for His kingdom purposes. This Greek word for holiness is used in 1 Timothy 2:15 and Romans 6:19,22, among other verses.

> *For God hath not called us unto uncleanness, but unto holiness.*
>
> 1 Thessalonians 4:7

However, holiness in Acts 3:12 is translated from the Greek word *eusebia,* which means a form of godliness that is evident in attitude and behavior.[3] While the Greek words often indicate more than one meaning, holiness continues to maintain a general meaning of being set aside for God's divine purpose.

With that understanding in mind and our denomination aside, we are a part of God's kingdom, and our kingdom passion demands that we live lives that are holy unto the Lord. A life of holiness releases the character and power of God into the earth. Therefore, holiness is not just for the Holiness denomination but for every believer because their image, reputation, and persona are the tools that God uses to minister Christ to the world.

Miracles in the New Testament is translated from two Greek words. The first is *dunamis,* which means to have power or inherent ability with supernatural origin.[4] The word *semeion* is translated "miracles" more often than *dunamis. Semeion* means a sign, a mark, or a token.[5] If we combine these two definitions, it is apparent that a miracle is God's supernatural power intervening in natural functions as a sign to believers and unbelievers that He is all-powerful.

What happened to the Church? In the early days she had passion for miracles to happen. In this day of knowledge and technology it seems that the Church has made religion so practical and ritualistic that many ministries no longer allow for the supernatural power of the Holy Spirit to intervene. This is not a picture of kingdom passion or Pentecost! We may have no power to program a miracle, but God has given us the authority to expect one. If there is a need in our lives, we are to expect God to meet it. Kingdom passion allows our needs and desires to be the seeds that produce a harvest of supernatural blessings in our lives and the lives of others.

We should always remember that a miracle is not something that stands by itself. It is a sign that God uses to prove His point about something else. That's why the Scriptures often make the distinction between signs and wonders. The sign is the occurrence of the miracle, and the wonder is the result of the miracle. For example, when a drug addict thinks he's going into a house to get another fix and enters a church gathering by accident, that is a miracle—a sign that the supernatural power of God is active and working at that moment. Then, when the drug addict leaves the church saved and determined to get off drugs, that is a wonder—we marvel at the supernatural power of God to change a person's life in a miraculous way.

When a person begins to speak in tongues that is a sign; but when that same person goes home and speaks to their spouse after giving them the silent treatment for the entire week, that is a wonder. When a believer who doesn't tithe is slain in the spirit, that is a sign; but when that same person gets up off the floor convinced they will never rob God again, that is a wonder. Miracles are not just something we marvel at; they are used by God for specific purposes. Believers with kingdom passion expect miracles to happen in their lives so that God's purposes can be accomplished. They understand that miracles are not only for the purpose of altering circumstances but also for the purpose of transforming lives.

Revelation might be the most essential of all components in the kingdom of God, and revelation was profoundly given on the Day of Pentecost. In simple terms, revelation is revealing something. In Scripture, revelation uncovers the mysteries of God. And revelation is intimately connected to vision. The profound and prolific writer Winifred Newman once stated, "Vision is the world's most desperate need."[6] Why is vision our most desperate need? We have no kingdom assignments without vision. And without vision, our kingdom assignments are

33

drudgery. A vision without task is a dream, but a task with vision is sure victory.

Although vision is critical and carries much weight; in order to develop, it has to be coupled with its cousin, revelation. Vision is what is seen; revelation is the reason God is showing it. In a mathematical problem, vision is the equation and revelation is the answer. Revelation gives clarity to any act or event that occurs in one's life.

Have you ever raised a question about something or someone in your life? Then five years later the Lord shows you exactly what you need to see to understand the person or situation. That's revelation. Have you ever had a question about why you found yourself in a difficult situation? Then a few weeks later the very thing you wondered about began to work for your good and you began to understand that what you went through then is working in your now. That's revelation.

Believers with kingdom passion know that their passion is fueled by a steady stream of revelation in their lives. And today is no exception, especially when there are so many questions about where God was on September 11, 2001, during the suicide bombings in the Holy Land, when a mother murdered her children, and why snipers took innocent lives. Revelation gives God's wisdom for the most perplexing questions of life.

How does revelation come into one's life? Spend time with God and allow Him to speak to you in prayer and through His Word. Make the Word applicable in your own life. Develop patience by waiting for God to confirm what He speaks in your spirit before making a move. Listen to the voices of wisdom—those older and more experienced believers in your life—and allow God to reveal some things to you through their experiences.

Pentecostalism breaks out in the kingdom when one develops passion for holiness, miracles, and revelation to manifest. But there is another key to experiencing Pentecost.

Be in the Right Place

Jesus told the disciples not to leave Jerusalem until they had received the promise of the Father (see Acts 1:4). So they gathered in the same Upper Room where Jesus had had communion with the twelve on that Thursday night before He was crucified. Many scholars and theologians believe that by giving the bread (His body) and the wine (His blood) to the disciples, He gave Himself away before He was taken to be crucified on Friday. Therefore, He gave Himself away during the first communion in the Upper Room; but during the next communion in the Upper Room (Pentecost), He put Himself back together again. The disciples were in the right place to have communion.

Pentecost is being in the place God called you to be in. Where is your Upper Room? That's where you will experience Pentecost, that is where you will have communion with the Holy Spirit, and that is where your kingdom passion will stay fired up. I am convinced that some of us never experience Pentecost because we are simply in the wrong place.

The church that has received the clarion call to do mission and outreach in the community where they exist but does nothing to fulfill this call is in the wrong place. The pastors who do not walk in the apostolic anointing and mantle placed upon them and follow the whims of their people rather than leading their congregations are in the wrong place. Any deacon, trustee, officer, or leader who does not support the vision of their apostle, bishop, or pastor and is hindering it is in the wrong place.

Believers who do not involve themselves in worship, Bible study, tithing, and missions are in the wrong place. A couple who lives together before the exchanging of marital vows before God is in the wrong place. A ten-year-old child who tells his forty-year-old parent what he will do and will not do is in the wrong place. And a brilliant and intelligent mind, standing on the corner selling crack cocaine, is clearly in the wrong place.

The right place is being in the will of God. The right place is where your spirit is fed God's Word, your soul finds restoration and peace, and you can hear from the Lord. The right place is in worship, where your spirit shouts and your face radiates joy and peace. The right place is where you study and meditate on God's Word, and God gives you a personal sermon just for your situation.

The right place could be while you are driving in your car, and all of a sudden you break into praise, right there at the stoplight. The right place could be when you walk on your treadmill or the track, and out of nowhere you just start thinking about the goodness of Jesus. It could be while you are having prayer with a friend on the telephone or that fifteen-minute break you get at work.

Be in the right place, and you will have communion with the Holy Ghost and experience Pentecost. When you center on the things of God, you are setting yourself up for God to bless you real good! Holiness, miracles, and revelation come into your life, and you will see God's kingdom manifest in ways you never could imagine.

5

THE PRIORITIES
OF PENTECOST

*T*here is a humorous story told about a man who read Acts 2:1, where it says, "they were all with one accord." This man went home and told his wife that there was a car in the Bible. She said, "Baby, there is no car in the Bible."

He said, "Yes, there is."

She said, "Where?"

He said, "In Acts, where it says on the day of Pentecost, they were all in *one accord*." He was talking about a Honda Accord, but being "in one accord" has nothing to do with a car!

Be in One Accord

If you want a Pentecostal experience to break out in your life, learn how to get in one accord with the Lord and then with His people. James Hudson Taylor once stated, "Do not have your concert first and tune your instruments afterward. Begin your day with God."[1] Priority says to tune the instruments first—come together in one accord—and then the concert will be a success. Some of us are trying to have a concert without first tuning our instruments.

We saw in the last chapter that a Pentecostal experience requires communion with the Holy Spirit, being in God's will and allowing Him to speak to you. If you are wondering why you haven't experienced Pentecost, why that job or that wholesome relationship has not come yet, why you are not at the next level of kingdom passion—maybe you need to get in one accord with God. And getting in one accord with God usually means putting away some things.

> *That ye put off concerning the former conversation the old man, which is corrupt according to the deceitful lusts;*
>
> *And be renewed in the spirit of your mind;*
>
> *And that ye put on the new man, which after God is created in righteousness and true holiness.*
>
> Ephesians 4:22-24

Putting off the old man and putting on the new man is a picture of kingdom passion at work. Consider what the disciples had to put away in order for them to be in one accord with Jesus. Peter had to put away his quick temper, which caused him to cut off the ear of one of the soldiers who came to arrest Jesus. James and John, the sons of Zebedee, had to put away their need for superiority because their mother had asked Jesus if they could sit on His left and His right in His kingdom. Phillip and Andrew had to put away some prejudice. They were raised in an environment where the question was repeated, "Can anything good come out of Nazareth?"

Thomas had to put away doubt, which had caused him to question Jesus' resurrection. James, Simon, Bartholomew, and Judas (not Iscariot but the son of James) had to put away fear. They were with the disciples who hid in Jerusalem, fearing that the Roman soldiers would do to them what they did to Jesus. Matthew, the treasurer of the group, had to put away his IRS mentality because he had been consumed with Mo' Money... Mo' Money...and Mo' Money!

The old man was put away and the new man was put on in order for them to come into one accord with God and with each other when they were in the Upper Room. Perhaps the reason that Pentecost hasn't happened in some of our lives is because we still have some lies to put away. We still have some jealousy, fear, and old lustful thoughts to put away. By clearing our spirits of this stuff and refusing to tote baggage too heavy for us to carry anymore, we come into one accord with God and place ourselves in position to experience Pentecost.

Worship

On the Day of Pentecost, they were all in one accord worshiping the risen Lord. Worship is part of the Pentecostal experience. The word *worship* comes from the word *worth-ship*. Somewhere in the development of the English language the "th" was removed, and now we just have "worship." I wish the "th" had remained because "worth" is vital and meaningful. I contend that some people don't worship the Lord because they don't realize the "worth" of the Lord. It is when you realize what He is worth—that He suffered, bled, and died to save you—that you can truly worship Him.

What is Jesus worth to you? Is having Him in your life worth going through some trials and tribulations? Giving up an ungodly lifestyle or habit? Putting away gossip, lying, self-gratification, and pride? Your perception of what Jesus is worth to you determines your kingdom passion to worship.

We praise God for what He has done, but we worship Him for who He is. Considering who God is, He is undisputedly worthy to be praised. Perhaps you are angry or disappointed with God for not doing what you wanted Him to do, answering your prayer for a mate, healing your loved one, or giving you the job you had your eyes on. Everyone has something that turned out differently from what they expected. But even if your dreams passed like vapor in the air, you should still worship Jehovah.

> *But the hour cometh, and now is, when the true worshipers shall worship the Father in spirit and in truth: for the Father seeketh such to worship him.*

> John 4:23

God is seeking those who will worship Him regardless of what He has or has not done. He may not answer all of our prayers, but there are some prayers that He did answer; and no matter what is going on in our lives, God is worthy of our praise and worship. We will spend now and eternity plumbing the depths of His worthiness and never get to the height, depth, breadth, or bottom of it. And wherever we are in our understanding of His worth, worshiping Him for who He is and praising Him for all He has done keeps us passionate for His kingdom.

My exhortation to you today is to make worship a priority. Worship Him in private and then come together in fellowship and worship Him corporately—both are necessary. Private worship blends into corporate worship. Let very little keep you from church services and make up in your mind that no attitude you encounter before church will keep you from going. But on the other hand, don't think that just because you're in church every week, you've done your time in worship. Remember, God is always seeking those who will worship Him—and He didn't say "in church."

Inform your family and friends that they should not disturb you when it's time for you to worship. Let your supervisor know that you can work any day of the week except the day you go to church. If they don't go for that, then you just show up to work and worship right there while you are typing on the computer, working the cash register, or changing oil in a car. Worship is too vital to your kingdom life to be taken lightly.

What really happens when we worship? We invite the Holy Spirit to rule and reign in our lives and in our services. Our focus is on Jesus instead of the famous guest speaker or church personalities. We create an environment that is warm and hospitable and all feel welcome, no matter what age, culture, color, or how they are dressed. The anointing is strong on the preaching, teaching, and singing. Worship brings the Pentecostal power of the Holy Spirit on the scene.

Study

A pastor told a fascinating story about a member of his congregation, who came up to him after a service and said, "I love it when you preach, but I really love it when you teach."

He said, "What is the difference?"

She said, "Well, when you preach, I see God hugging you; and when I see Him hugging you, I feel Him hugging me. But when you teach, you give me something to live by day-by-day."

It is essential that we continue preaching the gospel and lifting up Jesus before the people. Preaching keeps us motivated! And that is what Peter did on the Day of Pentecost, bringing in three thousand new converts from all over the world in one day. But what kept the Pentecostal fires burning in the believers *after* the Day of Pentecost? In Acts 2:42, the Bible tells us that all remained steadfast in the apostle's doctrine, which simply means teaching. They studied the teachings of the Word by the apostles. While the church is motivated, inspired, and grows as people are saved through the preaching ministry, it is the teaching ministry that makes disciples and enhances fellowship.

Furthermore, believers are more effective when they study the doctrines of their own covering. We know that all Scripture is given and inspired by God, but it can be interpreted in many ways. Therefore, every Christian must learn the doctrine of their covering, the church where they have covenanted to be a member. Why is this important? We live in a day in which major media airs the teachings of diverse doctrinal beliefs all day and all night. How are we to process all the teachings we hear? God leads us to the place where they are teaching what He wants us to know, and that should be our foundational study. We can then judge what we hear in light of the teaching of our apostles, bishops, pastors, and other leaders who constitute our covering.

Like the woman in the pastor's congregation, who sought understanding concerning the difference between preaching and teaching, we have something to rely on daily when we receive the teaching of God's Word. And we need something rock hard and firm to stand on when the storms come. I believe this is what the disciples were begging Jesus for when they were caught in a storm on the Sea of Galilee.

> And the same day, when the even was come, he saith unto them, Let us pass over unto the other side.
>
> And when they had sent away the multitude, they took him even as he was in the ship. And there were also with him other little ships.
>
> And there arose a great storm of wind, and the waves beat into the ship, so that it was now full.
>
> And he was in the hinder part of the ship, asleep on a pillow: and they awake him, and say unto him, Master, carest thou not that we perish?
>
> Mark 4:35-41

I heard a pastor comment once that there are merely three kinds of people in the world. "There are those that are headed for a storm, there are those that are in a storm, then there are those that are coming out of a storm."

All of us have to face storms. Storms interrupt peace in our homes, upset conditions in our workplaces, bring conflict to relationships, creep up and take a loved one away from us, and disrupt the unity of our congregations. Storms do arise, but take comfort. Jesus didn't say, "Y'all go over to the other side." He said, "Let us pass over unto the other side." The disciples were not alone in the storm and neither are we. We never need to feel forsaken, abandoned, cast away, lost, confused, powerless, and as if nobody cares. Why? Because Jesus is ever by our side, even in your storm.

> For he hath said, I will never leave thee, nor forsake thee....So that we may boldly say, The Lord is my helper.
>
> Hebrews 13:5,6

If Jesus knew that a storm would arise, why did He lead the disciples into it? Jesus wanted to teach His disciples something. He wanted to illustrate the lesson of faith that He had taught them just before they got into the boat. During the storm, in their desperation, I believe the disciples needed to know some things. Perhaps this is why they cried out, "Master, carest thou not that we perish?" (Mark 4:38). Notice that they called Him Master. They did not call Him Savior, Lord, Lamb of God, Chief Cornerstone, High Priest, King of the Universe, or even Jesus. Why Master? The Greek word translated Master is *diadaskulos*, which means teacher.[2] In the midst of the storm, the disciples cried out for their teacher.

They didn't call Him Savior because they weren't resisting a temptation to sin. They didn't call Him Lord because they weren't in a governmental dispute requiring judgment. They didn't call Him High Priest because they weren't trying to get into the Holy of Holies to have communion with God. They called Him Master because they didn't know what to do. They were in a storm and asked Jesus to get up and teach them how to deal with it. That is exactly why study is vital; all of us need to be taught how to handle the storms of life.

I became the pastor of the Union Baptist Church in 1999. Upon arriving there I began two Bible studies affectionately referred to as TNTs: Tuesday Noon Teaching and Tuesday Night Teaching. These Bible studies draw hundreds of people and serve as a model for many churches throughout the country. There are a few reasons why I believe this Bible study is effective. It has a catchy, marketable name. It is study of the Bible and not traditions of men. It is primarily taught by the pastor, who can impart vision along with the Word of God. It teaches relevant topics such as finances, relationships, spiritual warfare, the gifts of the Spirit, parenting, church order, and others. It offers separate Bible study classes for youth while the adult classes are in session, and we provide meals for families prior to the service.

> I beseech you therefore, brethren, by the mercies of God, that ye present your bodies a living sacrifice, holy, acceptable unto God, which is your reasonable service.

And be not conformed to this world: but be ye transformed by the renewing of your mind, that ye may prove what is that good, and acceptable, and perfect, will of God.

Romans 12:1,2

When so much attention and care is put into the study of God's Word (and it doesn't hurt to throw in some natural food as well!) the congregation will conform less and less to the world and be more and more transformed through the revelation of the Word of God. And, like the early church, believers will maintain the fires of Pentecost and keep their passion for God's kingdom. Then they will prove the good and acceptable and perfect will of God in their homes, churches, workplaces, and communities.

Fellowship

When the believers in the Upper Room came into one accord with the Holy Spirit on the Day of Pentecost, they came into one accord with each other. Then, after the Day of Pentecost, they kept their Pentecostal fervor burning brightly by continuing to fellowship with one another.

And they continued stedfastly in the apostles' doctrine and fellowship, and in breaking of bread, and in prayers.

Acts 2:42

The cross extends vertically *and* horizontally. The vertical extension of the cross symbolizes Jesus' relationship with the Father. The horizontal extension of the cross symbolizes His relationship with us. The cross is also a reminder to us that being in Christ means having a vertical relationship with God and a horizontal relationship with each other.

Godly relationships constitute the fiber and strength of the kingdom of God, and these relationships are formed and matured in and out of the church building. It's no mistake that the disciples of the first century church used breaking bread as an illustration. I discovered the power of breaking bread in the development of relationship when we included a meal before our Bible studies. The benefits were manifold in that parents did not have to cook, children received a balanced meal, and only the people assigned to serve and clean up had to do so. But these were not the most important blessings.

As people fellowshipped over a meal, they got to know one another and relationships began to develop. Members of our church who worshiped together on Sunday but sat on opposite sides of the sanctuary were talking to one another and sharing together. Their fellowship carried over into the worship services, so that they were no longer worshiping with strangers but with those who knew their story.

Therefore, I urge churches to begin eating more! Not for the food but for the fellowship. And if one of your members complains about using the tithes and offerings for the meals, just take them to the book of Acts and let them see for themselves how to experience Pentecost for real!

Evangelism

Another priority that comes to us from the very birth of the Church at Pentecost is evangelism. While attending a conference, I heard one of the lecturers state, "In many instances we have been concerned about how many people we are getting in church, but very few churches ever measure how many people they are sending out of the church."

After hearing that, you might immediately raise the question, "Why would anyone want to send someone out of the church?" Well, we are not talking about sending people out in the way of excommunication or expulsion from fellowship. That is certainly not something we pray for! However, we are to be sending believers out into the highways and byways to compel unbelievers to believe, to encourage the lost to be saved.

Pentecost is synonymous with evangelism because the saints immediately hit the street, Peter preached the gospel, and three thousand were saved in the first day. Therefore, kingdom passion embraces and promotes evangelism. After our Upper Room experience in our church services, we are to hit the streets and induce others to be saved and come into the family of God.

My definition of evangelism is the ministering of the gospel for the purpose of a person developing a wholesome and lasting relationship with Jesus Christ. Evangelism is reaching beyond ourselves to expand the kingdom of God. It is making the last commandment of Jesus our first priority.

Go ye therefore, and teach all nations, baptizing them in the name of the Father, and of the Son, and of the Holy Ghost.

Matthew 28:19

In his book, *African-American Church Growth,* Carlyle Stewart says, "The recent proliferation of church literature on evangelism as a tool for church growth attests to its importance. Few churches today have instituted prophetic evangelism programs designed to bring persons to Christ. We live in an age where churches do not invite people to church and don't have systematic visitation programs to tell people the Good News of the gospel."³

If what Mr. Stewart is saying is true, then the Church at large in America is not experiencing Pentecost. We are not going out from our church services to bring the Good News of Jesus Christ to our families, neighbors, co-workers, and friends. I believe we need a revelation of what it is to be spiritually dead to renew our kingdom passion for evangelism. When we look at our unsaved loved ones and those unbelievers around us and understand that they are spiritually dead and destined for an eternity separated from God and us, we will get motivated and fired up to evangelize!

This is best illustrated in John 11, when Jesus received word from Mary and Martha, the sisters of Lazarus, that their brother was seriously ill.

Now a certain man was sick, named Lazarus, of Bethany, the town of Mary and her sister Martha.

(It was that Mary which anointed the Lord with ointment, and wiped his feet with her hair, whose brother Lazarus was sick.)

Therefore his sisters sent unto him, saying, Lord, behold, he whom thou lovest is sick.

When Jesus heard that, he said, This sickness is not unto death, but for the glory of God, that the Son of God might be glorified thereby.

John 11:1-4

Jesus sent word back to them that this sickness was not unto death, and instead of running to Lazarus' bedside to heal him, He stayed right where He was for two days and did nothing. This was fine with the disciples because Jesus had become a marked man and many people were trying to find Him in order to stone Him. However, after the two days passed Jesus suddenly decided to go to Bethany in Judea to tend to His beloved friend, Lazarus. The disciples questioned the wisdom of His decision and Jesus answered them in a way they did not anticipate.

Then after that saith he to his disciples, Let us go into Judaea again.

His disciples say unto him, Master, the Jews of late sought to stone thee; and goest thou thither again?

Jesus answered, Are there not twelve hours in the day? If any man walk in the day, he stumbleth not, because he seeth the light of this world.

But if a man walk in the night, he stumbleth, because there is no light in him.

These things said he: and after that he saith unto them, Our friend Lazarus sleepeth; but I go, that I may awake him out of sleep.

Then said his disciples, Lord, if he sleep, he shall do well.

Howbeit Jesus spake of his death: but they thought that he had spoken of taking of rest in sleep.

Then said Jesus unto them plainly, Lazarus is dead.

And I am glad for your sakes that I was not there, to the intent ye may believe; nevertheless let us go unto him.

John 11:7-15

First of all, Jesus said that Lazarus would not die, but what we find is that Lazarus did die. Did Jesus pervert truth and lie to Mary and Martha? No, Jesus did not lie because no lie can be found in Him. The answer to our question is found in verses 9 and 10, where Jesus explained to His disciples that you are can be physically alive and spiritually dead or you can be physically dead but spiritually alive. Jesus understood that there are two kinds of death. There is a physical death, and there is a spiritual death. He was telling the disciples that Lazarus was physically dead but spiritually alive.

People who do not know Jesus Christ as Savior and Lord are physically alive but spiritually dead. They are walking around in the darkness, stumbling, with no light in them. But believers, when they die, may be physically dead but they are spiritually alive. Paul refers to them as a great cloud of witnesses in Hebrews 12:1. From this truth we find our spiritual point of reference for evangelism. We are to win the souls of those who are physically alive but spiritually dead so that, when their dying day comes, they will be physically dead but spiritually alive.

But what does passion for kingdom evangelism look like? Again, Pentecost is our first model. Pentecost was radical. Believers hit the street on fire to be fruitful and multiply, to bring more followers to Jesus, more sons to God the Father, and give the Holy Spirit more people to inhabit, purify, and work through to see even more people saved.

In our ministry we have an annual revival called "The Shekinah Glory Revival." This week is packed with activities such as a classical music and dance presentation, a community parade, church and political leaders' luncheon, and dynamic preaching and teaching with some of the best voices in the nation. We top it off with a black-tie gala concert and reception with fireworks that symbolizes the revival bringing light to the city. This revival is full of holiness, miracles, and revelation. It is a Pentecostal experience.

During our revival in 1999, we had a week of souls getting blessed, delivered, and set free, but on the Sunday following there was something still longing in my soul. It occurred to me that in Acts 2, not only did the disciples get revived on the day of Pentecost, but after their revival in the Holy Ghost, they went out telling the wonderful things of God. I realized that that is what was missing. We revived, but we had not gone out anywhere to invite others to be revived.

On that Sunday we had a "revival after the revival." After the 9:00 A.M. service, I asked for thirty people to meet me to receive a kingdom assignment. In fifteen minutes I directed them to go out and minister Jesus Christ to people in the homeless shelter, soup kitchen, AIDS home, a local street corner, and anyone the Holy Spirit led them to minister to. I gave simple instructions on how to communicate the plan of salvation, and equipped them concerning what to expect and how to handle dangerous situations. Then they left on fire. Two hours later they returned for our second service with more fire. This impromptu evangelistic team led seventeen souls to Jesus Christ that Sunday.

I believe God said, "Amen," to this effort. They brought back with them a young man from the homeless shelter. He asked me if he could say something at the end of the service and I consented. That young man took the microphone, and his testimony convicted me and everybody sitting in that church. He said, "I'm so glad this morning somebody came and got me, because I always knew the Lord had a plan for my life. I was just waiting on the church to come and give it to me."

This is our charge for kingdom evangelism: "I was just waiting on the church to come and give it to me." Someone is waiting on you to come and give them the plan. Wherever you go, share the plan, whether you are at work, in the grocery store, at the Laundromat, at your family reunion, or at your auxiliary meeting. Wherever you go, be passionate to share the Good News with those who are stumbling in darkness.

The priorities of Pentecost are to stay in one accord with God and with believers, to worship Him in Spirit and in truth, to study to show yourself approved, to not forsake the fellowship of other believers, and to do the work of an evangelist. If you will keep these Pentecostal priorities in your life, you will find that your passion for God's kingdom continues to grow and flourish.

6

THE POWER OF PENTECOST

While pastoring the New Hope Granville Baptist Church in North Carolina, we experienced a terrible hurricane named Fran, which caused tremendous damage. Power lines fell all around the church, and the night before Sunday service, one of my members called and said, "There is no way we can have service."

I asked "Why?"

She said, "There is no power in the church. The lines are down, and there ain't no power."

I said to her gently, "Sister, let me for a moment correct you. You mean, there is no *electricity* in the church, but there ought to be some *power* there because our power is not hooked up to a power line, but we got power in the name of Jesus."

Now I understood clearly what she was saying, but I also wanted her to know the difference between electricity and the *dunamis* power of God—power that causes the holiness, miracles, and revelation of Pentecost to break out. After all, what is Pentecost without power? And what is power without Pentecost?

In essence, this exposition is incomplete if we don't consider the Pentecostal priority of God's power. I'm dedicating an entire chapter to the power of Pentecost because the power of God is the lifeblood of the Church.

After Jesus was resurrected, He went up to the Mount of Olives. There, He lifted His hands and blessed the disciples who were present. The Bible says that after He ascended and went up into the clouds, most of the disciples disbanded and went their own ways. But we know that some of them went back to Jerusalem, where Jesus had told them to go, and waited for the promise of the Father.

> *And, being assembled together with them, [Jesus] commanded them that they should not depart from Jerusalem, but wait for the promise of the Father, which, saith he, ye have heard of me.*
>
> *For John truly baptized with water; but ye shall be baptized with the Holy Ghost not many days hence.*
>
> *When they therefore were come together, they asked of him, saying, Lord, wilt thou at this time restore again the kingdom to Israel?*
>
> *And he said unto them, It is not for you to know the times or the seasons, which the Father hath put in his own power.*
>
> *But ye shall receive power, after that the Holy Ghost is come upon you: and ye shall be witnesses unto me both in Jerusalem, and in all Judaea, and in Samaria, and unto the uttermost part of the earth.*
>
> *And when he had spoken these things, while they beheld, he was taken up; and a cloud received him out of their sight.*
>
> Acts 2:4-9 [Insert mine]

It is interesting that the disciples are still asking Jesus when He will restore the kingdom of Israel. Jesus tells them that the times and seasons for the shifts of natural kingdoms are in the Father's hands, not theirs. Then He goes on to say that the power they will receive is the power of the Holy Ghost, which will compel them to be a witness for Him from their homes to the uttermost parts of the earth.

The promise is significant because it is directly correlated with the power of Pentecost. The disciples were not as clear about the promise then as we are now. Perhaps they thought that the promise was that Jesus would show up again in bodily form. This is not so far removed from a possibility because the angels had told them this was going to occur after Jesus ascended.

> *And while they looked stedfastly toward heaven as he went up, behold, two men stood by them in white apparel;*
>
> *Which also said, Ye men of Galilee, why stand ye gazing up into heaven? this same Jesus, which is taken up from you into heaven, shall so come in like manner as ye have seen him go into heaven.*
>
> Acts 1:10,11

Before we attack the disciples for their expectation that what Jesus was referring to as the promise of the Father was His bodily return, please remember that we live in a world of high-level marketing, this generation of "show me the money" and "I'll believe it when I see it." We want our five physical senses to verify everything so much that we often reduce the very presence of the Holy Spirit to the tangible, the mundane, and the physical. It is this expectation of and emphasis on the kingdom being developed and enhanced by physical things that forces me to confront what I believe to be a skewed perspective on prosperity and blessing. I am referring to a teaching that has swept our country and others that declares that we can "will" prosperity and everything we desire and need into our lives.

Pentecostal Prosperity

Building an entire structure of thought from 3 John 2, "Beloved, I wish above all things that thou mayest prosper and be in health, even as thy soul prospereth," many teachers distort and pervert the power of God into satisfying greed and rationalizing covetousness. While God truly intends for us to prosper and be in good health, some preachers and teachers use this principle with reckless abandonment, making it the primary focus and intent for God's people. In some churches and ministries, the issue of prosperity has taken priority over evangelism and discipleship, which is just as dangerous as not mentioning the principle of prosperity at all.

This destructive tendency in the body of Christ became real when I heard a popular minister on Christian television who, after teaching his congregation several good points about prosperity, pushed the principle to the extreme by vigorously equating a very expensive material possession, a Rolex watch, with a blessing of God. This kind of teaching distorts the divine intent and purpose for prosperity. Prosperity is part of our destiny, but it is not for us to show off and boast about. The divine intent for prosperity is that God get the glory and that we reinvest our financial blessing into the kingdom so that His covenant can be established in the earth. Like the power of God, the prosperity of God is a means to an end. When we make the means our end, we pervert the divine intention and a malignancy forms in the kingdom of God.

The root problem with this particular teaching on prosperity is that it exalts the tangible blessings of God over the spiritual blessings of God. I believe that all blessings begin in the spirit realm and then manifest into the tangible realm. It is in the spirit that I am blessed with an expectation, a divine right to possess what God has given me, and a peace about the possession—all because I am His son. He has adopted me, made me accepted in the Beloved, predestinated me, and given me a hope and a future for good and not evil. When I truly understand the seat of my spiritual blessing, I am continuously aware that all natural blessings flow from my spiritual relationship with and position in Jesus Christ. Whatever I obtain in the physical, I have already been blessed and fulfilled in the spirit.

A good illustration of this would be if my natural father were a millionaire. As his son I have the resources to purchase any kind of car I desire. However much I enjoy and am grateful for the car, every time I drive it or look at it or think about it I am overwhelmed by the true blessing, which is having a father who has the ability and the desire to bless me, who has given me the right to use his resources. In fact, the physical is subordinate to the spiritual in every area and from every perspective of my life.

A biblical illustration is found in Luke 8, when Jesus healed the woman with the issue of blood. Do you remember what He said to her?

> And he said unto her, Daughter, be of good comfort: thy faith hath made thee whole; go in peace.
>
> Luke 8:48

Jesus clearly declares that nothing physical, including Himself, healed her. Her faith made her whole, and faith is a spiritual substance, according to Hebrews 11:1.

Why is this so important? The expensive item the preacher on television had was not the blessing; the spiritual relationship the preacher had with the Father who blessed him with the item was the blessing. A drug dealer and a pimp can possess similar items. But for a child of God, any natural blessing is appreciated in the context of the spiritual blessing, the eternal relationship with the Father.

Sometimes it takes a while for the spiritual blessing to manifest the natural blessing. A good example of this is when Daniel prayed for twenty-one days for a breakthrough and nothing happened. Just when he was getting discouraged God sent an angel to tell him why there was a delay.

> And he said unto me, O Daniel, a man greatly beloved, understand the words that I speak unto thee, and stand upright: for unto thee am I now sent. And when he had spoken this word unto me, I stood trembling.
>
> Then said he unto me, Fear not, Daniel: for from the first day that thou didst set thine heart to understand, and to chasten

thyself before thy God, thy words were heard, and I am come for thy words.

But the prince of the kingdom of Persia withstood me one and twenty days: but, lo, Michael, one of the chief princes, came to help me; and I remained there with the kings of Persia.

Daniel 10:11-13

The delay was caused by a spiritual battle in heaven between God's angel, who was sent to bring the answer to Daniel's prayers, and the demonic authority in Persia. Daniel couldn't get his breakthrough in the physical until some battles were first won in the spiritual. I believe the television preacher knows these things, but he grossly misrepresented them. And I was further vexed because this was broadcast all over the world.

I wonder what they thought about God and a Rolex watch in Somalia. The church in America must be careful not to insult the people of God in other countries. What is considered a blessing to me will not be a blessing to a Somalian. A Rolex watch means nothing to an undernourished mother who has nothing to feed her children. Furthermore, the watch may cost ten thousand dollars in America, but the people in some third world country who made the watch were only paid fifty cents for a day's work. To them, an American preacher holding up a Rolex watch they made for little earnings is more a symbol of financial rape than a blessing from God.

The church in America is often guilty of what poet, author, and sociologist of religion, C. Eric Lincoln, calls "Americanity." During a class I attended at Duke University, he purported that

Americanity is America's definition of success and achievement understood in the context of Christianity. History will record that for many people in America, the American dream has become an American nightmare because systems have been established that will not allow every citizen to get wealthy. While I believe in the favor of God and that the wealth of the wicked is stored up for the righteous (see Prov. 13:22), I also believe we must be cautious in teaching that everyone in the kingdom of God will be rich financially. In truth, the American system is not established to achieve that reality.

There must be what I like to call "Transitory Prosperity." Transitory Prosperity is the idea of prosperity being distributed into every area of life, not just the arena of finances. We must be prosperous in education, the family, community involvement, social and political action, church membership, empowerment, and other areas as well. Transitory Prosperity applies the spiritual wealth of heaven to everyday difficulties, thus giving God free rein to work all things together for our good.

Transitory Prosperity says that I may not have a job, but I have the mind of Christ (see 1 Cor. 2:16). Transitory Prosperity says that my marriage may be on the brink of a break up, but Jesus upholds all things by the word of His power (see Heb. 1:3). Transitory Prosperity says that I may not be in my dream house yet, but God gives me the desires of my heart because I delight in Him (see Ps. 37:4). Transitory Prosperity is prosperity transitioned from the spirit realm to the natural realm—and that is the power of prosperity experienced in Pentecost.

The Power of Tongues

Going back to the beginning of our discussion in this chapter, the disciples were expecting Jesus to show up physically on the day of Pentecost. Instead, He sent the promise of the Father to them, just has He had spoken to them before He was crucified.

> *But the Comforter, which is the Holy Ghost, whom the Father will send in my name, he shall teach you all things, and bring all things to your remembrance, whatsoever I have said unto you.*
>
> John 14:26

> *Nevertheless I tell you the truth; It is expedient for you that I go away: for if I go not away, the Comforter will not come unto you; but if I depart, I will send him unto you.*
>
> John 16:7

The Day of Pentecost went far beyond their expectations when the Holy Spirit came into the Upper Room like a mighty rushing wind, set tongues of fire upon their heads, and they began speaking with other tongues. But the power of the Holy Spirit did not stop there because God never releases His power without a task. Don't ask God for His power if you don't have a kingdom purpose for it! In this day especially, when terrorism seeks to destroy the innocent and good, when corruption runs rampant in governments and corporations, when media pours out pornography and foul language; we need the power of the Holy Ghost to radically transform our generation.

Our model is Pentecost. God poured out His Spirit for a reason. The believers began speaking with other tongues for a reason.

> And they were all filled with the Holy Ghost, and began to speak with other tongues, as the Spirit gave them utterance.
>
> And there were dwelling at Jerusalem Jews, devout men, out of every nation under heaven.
>
> Now when this was noised abroad, the multitude came together, and were confounded, because that every man heard them speak in his own language.
>
> And they were all amazed and marvelled, saying one to another, Behold, are not all these which speak Galilaeans?
>
> And how hear we every man in our own tongue, wherein we were born?

> Acts 2:4-8

The Greek word translated "tongues" in verse 8 is *dialektos*. This is where we get the word "dialect," and it refers to the language of an ethnic people or a province.[1] There is a dispute among Bible scholars about this. Some believe the believers spoke in the languages of all the devout Jews from every nation. Others believe that they spoke in tongues and the devout Jews from every nation simply *heard* their own language spoken because in verse 4 the Greek word for tongues is *glossa*, which simply means tongue (including the organ of the body) or speech.[2] Either way, the power of the Holy Spirit moved through a bunch of Galilaeans to speak in tongues as a miraculous sign to the unbelieving devout Jews from every nation.

Paul mentions this later in 1 Corinthians 14:22, where he says, "Wherefore tongues are for a sign, not to them that believe, but to them that believe not."

The Upper Room experience of speaking in tongues brings a believer into communion with the Holy Ghost, just as the believers did on the Day of Pentecost. Commonly referred to as a believer's "prayer language," this tongue is spoken for purposes of communication with God and not men. Speaking in tongues builds up believers in their most holy faith (see Jude 20) and brings the Holy Spirit on the scene to impart revelation and understanding of God's Word and will for their lives.

The Upper Room experience of Pentecost is where kingdom passion is caught, and kingdom passion always compels us to move out and impart what we have received to others. In worship services, tongues becomes a gift of the Holy Spirit to impart edification, knowledge, and understanding. This is why Paul connects tongues with interpretation. When the Holy Spirit moves on a believer in fellowship to speak in a tongue, He always gives either that person or another believer the interpretation so that the entire congregation or group knows what God is saying to them.

The power of tongues for the Church is that this Pentecostal experience brings believers into the unity of the Spirit. God birthed the Church as a unified body in the Upper Room; and when they went out onto the streets, He maintained that unity as He added three thousand souls to the kingdom. How did He do this? Through tongues! They all understood what He was saying in their own languages. Through the supernatural mani-festation of tongues, He unified us and keeps us unified.

Again, I believe it is ironic and sad that the very thing God did—the precious promise that He kept—on the Day of Pentecost, which brought the power of the Holy Spirit and speaking in tongues to the Church, is one of the most divisive issues in the Church today. Furthermore, many of the denomi-nations who have supposedly been operating in the power of Pentecost for years are filled with lifeless traditions of men and women with little evidence of the power of God in which they were birthed.

There is no doubt in my mind and heart that the entire body of Christ needs a new revelation and experience of Pentecost. For some it will kindle their kingdom passion and for others it will add oxygen to the flame. But most important, it will bring us back into the unity and power of the Spirit.

Proverbs 18:21 tells us, "Death and life are in the power of the tongue." Though we may not speak in the tongues repre-sented on the day of Pentecost, we do have an obligation to use our tongue to speak life into the lives of many—saved and unsaved. I would like to call this the "edifying tongue." It is this tongue that brings liberation to the Church because it reflects the example of unity that Pentecost modeled.

All of us can talk about the wonderful works of God, which ultimately edify God and the Church. Paul says in 1 Corinthians 14:18 NASB, "I thank God, I speak in tongues more than you all;

however, in the church I desire to speak five words with my mind, that I might instruct others also, rather than ten thousand words in a tongue." This is called the edifying tongue, simply because wherever you go, there should be a word about the wonderful things of God spoken in your own language.

If you go to work, you may have the opportunity to speak in this tongue; if you are on the basketball court, you may have the opportunity to speak in this tongue; if you are in the grocery store, you have the opportunity to speak in this tongue. A testimony should always rest in your spirit about what God has done in your life. Americans may speak this tongue in English, the Hispanics may speak this tongue in Spanish, Africans may speak this tongue in Swahili, and the Japanese may speak this tongue in Japanese. It is a tongue in your own language. So open your mouth and speak! It is when you open your mouth and speak the wonderful things of God that a real sense of kingdom passion breaks out because God is getting the glory.

7

THE KINGDOM OF GOD IS RADICAL

W*ebster's New World College Dictionary* gives the following definition of "radical."

> 1 a) of or from the root or roots; going to the foundation or source of something; fundamental; basic [*a radical principle*] b)extreme; thorough [*a radical change in one's life*] 2 a) favoring fundamental or extreme change.[1]

Radicalism is often seen as being rebellious in the body of Christ. Although radicalism can be perverted into rebellion, from this definition radicalism is defeating that which is *not* fundamentally or basically right by establishing that which *is* fundamentally or basically right. What a picture of the kingdom of God invading and defeating the kingdom of darkness!

The kingdom of God is radical because it is *God's* kingdom, and He is the root and beginning of all creation. God is the most radical being in the universe. His kingdom is radical because it is His governmental structure of all knowledge, all experience, all faith, and all works that concern His people. Furthermore, the radical revelation of the kingdom of God is fundamental, basic, extreme, and thorough—and our lives are continuously changed as we walk in it. In a sense, from the moment we receive that radical revelation, we are engaged in bringing about fundamental or extreme change in the earth by manifesting God's kingdom.

Being a radical believer means having a passion and a determination to do and be what God has commanded in order to manifest His kingdom in the earth. As we saw in the first chapters, this involves learning to think like God thinks and do things God's way. We are literally governed by His Word and His Spirit, and this involves intense discipleship.

While it is most important to make things happen in the kingdom, it is also important to bring understanding to the people who are making things happen—which is discipleship. Kingdom principles and processes must be taught; otherwise, the vision and how that vision is to be carried out can be misunderstood and even rejected.

We know the religious Pharisees and Sadduccees were shocked and offended when Jesus began teaching about the kingdom of God, but the disciples struggled with these new, radical concepts also. We find an illustration of this in Luke 17, where Jesus has a dialogue with them about the necessity of forgiveness.

> *Take heed to yourselves: If thy brother trespass against thee, rebuke him; and if he repent, forgive him.*

And if he trespass against thee seven times in a day, and seven times in a day turn again to thee, saying, I repent; thou shalt forgive him.

And the apostles said unto the Lord, Increase our faith.

Luke 17:3-5

The disciples had such a problem with forgiveness that they asked Jesus to increase their faith! They probably had severe trouble with this initially because in the Old Testament only God could forgive sins and trespasses. That's why the religious Jews were so astounded and enraged when Jesus forgave someone's sin. By doing so, He was declaring that He was God. Then, in this passage in Luke, He carries this "heresy" one step further and commands the disciples that *they* were to forgive others also. This was so amazing and radical that they cried, "Increase our faith!" If Jesus made such a radical approach to addressing the forgiveness of sin, we also must be radical and work against the ungodly traditions that hinder the advancement of the kingdom in this regard.

Later in the text, God sets up a situation for the disciples to see where they should be in their faith walk. This passage of Scripture also illustrates some valuable kingdom principles for us today.

And it came to pass, as he went to Jerusalem, that he passed through the midst of Samaria and Galilee.

And as he entered into a certain village, there met him ten men that were lepers, which stood afar off:

And they lifted up their voices, and said, Jesus, Master, have mercy on us.

And when he saw them, he said unto them, Go show yourselves unto the priests. And it came to pass, that, as they went, they were cleansed.

Luke 17:11-14

Jesus was passing through Samaria in particular because the Jews and the Samaritans had no dealings. But it was destined that He and the disciples pass through Samaria because ten lepers were in need of healing and deliverance. When the lepers began to ask Jesus for healing, He told them to show themselves to the Jewish priests. This was necessary because, according to the Law, the priest was the one who determined a healing had taken place.

And one of them, when he saw that he was healed, turned back, and with a loud voice glorified God,

And fell down on his face at his feet, giving him thanks: and he was a Samaritan.

And Jesus answering said, Were there not ten cleansed? but where are the nine?

There are not found that returned to give glory to God, save this stranger.

And he said unto him, Arise, go thy way: thy faith hath made thee whole.

Luke 17:15-19

In route to the Jewish priests, the lepers realized they were cleansed and whole. We are not told how many went to the priest, but we are told that only one of the lepers, the Samaritan, returned to Jesus to glorify God. Within this miracle account are four radical principles of the kingdom of God to help us in our kingdom work.

Radical Principle #1
Your Life Is a Lesson to Others

The miracle that took place among the lepers was not just to bless the lepers. This miracle happened for the disciples' sake as well. They had asked Jesus to increase their faith, and that was exactly what Jesus did. He healed the ten lepers because miracles always increase a believer's faith. He also healed them as a demonstration of where the disciples' faith should be and what that kind of faith could do in their lives. With this interpretation, you might say the lepers were healed to teach the disciples a lesson. As Jesus did what He was called to do in His life, others around Him learned about God's kingdom and how it operates.

There are times when the Holy Spirit will use your life as a lesson for someone else. He might do exceedingly, abundantly above all that you ask or think for you and for those who are walking with you. There are times God will openly reward you, so that He can get open glory. There are moments when God will bless you, so that even unbelievers can know that there is a God and He is all-powerful. Many of the experiences that we go through are lessons about the kingdom learned by others.

To take this a step further, having passion for the kingdom involves sharing your stories and testimonies. Too many times

Christians are silent about the mighty works or the seemingly small but powerfully significant works of God. But in actuality, one of the best sermons, teachings, evangelistic strategies, and ministry opportunities is simply you telling your story.

> *For thou, O God, hast proved us: thou hast tried us, as silver is tried.*
>
> *Thou broughtest us into the net; thou laidst affliction upon our loins.*
>
> *Thou hast caused men to ride over our heads; we went through fire and through water: but thou broughtest us out into a wealthy place.*
>
> Psalm 66:10-12

Wouldn't it be a tragedy if you were tried as silver (in fire) to be placed in a net (resources tied up), afflictions upon your loins (unexpected trials), men to ride over your head (people taking advantage of you), go through fire and through water (dangerous situations), and then God brought you out into a wealthy place (a place of peace, prosperity, promotion, and power)—and you never told anyone about it. No one would learn the lessons you learned, gain the wisdom you gained, see the experience through your eyes, or be strengthened by your encouraging resolve. What a misfortune!

God does not bring us through the tests, trials, and tribulations of life into a wealthy place for our sakes alone. He uses our lives as lessons for everyone He has connected to us. We all have a kingdom assignment to go and teach someone else about the glorious abilities of God.

Radical Principle #2
Radical Obedience Receives Raging Criticism

And Jesus answering said, Were there not ten cleansed? but where are the nine?

There are not found that returned to give glory to God, save this stranger.

And he said unto him, Arise, go thy way: thy faith hath made thee whole.

Luke 17:15-19

I was a child who grew up in the church, and through the years as this story was preached, I heard the saints criticize these lepers. I have heard many preachers, Sunday school teachers, and church members talk about what a shame it was for those other nine lepers not to come back to Jesus to say thank you. Oh yes, only an ignorant, old Samaritan came back to give glory to God and thank Jesus for His healing.

The other nine lepers have been evaluated, labeled, and criticized for their actions—all based on the assumption that chastisement and disapproval were behind Jesus' questions, "Were there not ten cleansed? but where are the nine?" However, if you really consider the details of Jesus' instructions to the ten lepers, He never told them to return to Him. He simply said, "Go show yourselves unto the priests," which is what they did. I believe this is a case where criticism is unjustly given. And, it struck me that criticism came when the lepers were just doing what Jesus told them to do.

If you are filled with passion for the kingdom of God and are faithfully doing what God has called you to do, then you are going to encounter criticism—from within the Church and outside of the Church. In fact, the most grievous and challenging criticism you will receive will be from those closest to you. My counsel to you after years of ministry is that you cannot stop because of criticism. You must forgive, and if the one who is being critical and judgmental refuses to reconcile with you, you must kick the dust off your feet and move on with God.

In truth, being criticized contains good information for anyone who is serious about doing kingdom work because the accuser of the brethren, who incites criticism and judgmentalism between brothers and sisters or from outside the Church, usually does this when we step out and are faithful to complete our kingdom assignments. When you heed the clarion call to provide a safe place for the abused, food and shelter for the homeless, and minister the gospel to prostitutes, drug addicts, and others who are unsaved and uncared for, prepare to be criticized and decide to rejoice in it. If God be for you, who can be against you?

In my years of ministry, I have learned the benefits of criticism.

- Criticism is often a sign that you are accomplishing something for the kingdom of God.

- Criticism is an indication that you are retrieving someone or something for God's kingdom that the enemy doesn't want to give up.

- Criticism not only hones your skills in spiritual warfare, but it helps to clarify and establish your purpose and priorities.

- Criticism is a great purifier that separates you from those things that are not of God and those people who are not called to the same kingdom mission that He has called you to accomplish.

- Criticism can be based on truth, and when the Holy Spirit uses criticism to convict you of sin, error, or wrong thinking, you can correct these areas and move on with greater joy, wisdom, and power to carry out your kingdom assignments.

This is not the season for you to get discouraged because you are being criticized for doing what Jesus told you to do. This is the season for you to endure, remain steadfast, and know that God is sending you some vision catchers and people who will help you in the mission. Consider the influence you will have if you just press beyond where you are. Think of the many people you will bless if you don't allow the few that don't agree with you to stop you. First John 4:4 says, "Greater is he that is in you, than he that is in the world." Kingdom living may put you in the line of fire most of the time, but you remain in the safe haven of the secret place of the Most High God. Therefore, never forget that radical criticism should never hinder radical obedience.

Radical Principle #3
Justified Disobedience

If the lepers were being obedient and doing what Jesus told them to do, then we must conclude that the leper who came back to Jesus was also disobedient. What?! This is the hero preachers, teachers, and church members lift up as being a model for saying thank you! Yes. He was the disobedient one because Jesus had told the lepers, "Go show yourselves unto the priests." But the Samaritan returned to Jesus. Consequently, he was disobedient to the commandment of the Lord—and yet he glorified God.

The Samaritan's disobedience was not a disobedience to defy God but to glorify God. Dr. Martin Luther King Jr. would have called this "civil disobedience." Gandhi would have called this "moral order." And Nelson Mandela would have said that it was right on time! It was a disobedience that was a foreshadowing of how the blood of Jesus Christ shed on the cross would cause God's old system of the Law to be replaced by His new system of grace. The Samaritan's act of worship and relationship to Jesus was a type of the New Testament sonship believers enjoy today. Therefore, we can safely call this "justified disobedience."

Justified disobedience is standing against the evil systems of the day by doing things God's way. These evil systems constitute racism, poverty, homelessness, and any shameful condition that does not bring glory to God's kingdom. There are many churches, pastors, and Christians who have been grossly criticized for getting involved in political affairs and the systems that govern us, but many of our people are suffering as a result of the lack of godly order and morality in these areas. This criticism, of course, has come from a warped theology that the Church should not be involved with politics and government. However, you cannot be kingdom-minded and not have a passion for addressing the issues that affect the Church and its people.

We must always consider the relevance of our ministry. Some ministries are so prophetic and consumed with addressing such areas as politics, community affairs, social conditions, and world problems that they fail to create an atmosphere for charismatic worship. On the other hand, there are some charismatic ministries that are so consumed with operating in the anointing and allowing the Spirit to flow freely that they ignore matters like racism, sexism, crime, and even the homeless. While both prophetic and charismatic focuses are vital parts to any ministry, it is the challenge of a kingdom ministry to have a balance of the two. I call this being "Prophecharismatic."

Prophecharismatic is a word that I use in the ministry at Union Baptist Church to describe the old cliché that we "cannot be so heavenly bound (charismatic) that we are no earthly good (prophetic)." Any ministry that is serious about developing passion for the kingdom must operate in both these areas of ministry to be successful.

Another way of looking at this is our model of the cross. We have the vertical relationship (charismatic) and the horizontal relationship (prophetic). Often when our churches or ministries are not accustomed to either the charismatic or the prophetic, rejecting that with which they are not comfortable, justified disobedience may occur to bring the changes needed for that church or ministry to become effective.

If you have a passion to help make life better for someone else by going into public service in government or a social service organization, you may be labeled rebellious and disobedient by those who believe that the only kingdom assignments believers have are to pray, study God's Word, and lead people to Jesus. But the Bible says,

> *Hereby perceive we the love of God, because he laid down his life for us: and we ought to lay down our lives for the brethren.*
>
> *But whoso hath this world's good, and seeth his brother have need, and shutteth up his bowels of compassion from him, how dwelleth the love of God in him?*
>
> *My little children, let us not love in word, neither in tongue; but in deed and in truth.*
>
> 1 John 3:16-18

Kingdom passion often involves doing things that the Church's legalistic order of the day would dictate not to do. The apostles of the book of Acts were trailblazers, always doing things that were unprecedented in ministry as the Holy Spirit and the Word of God dictated. When a believer does not just follow the regimen of going to church and being involved in the traditional ministries of prayer, singing in the choir, distributing food and clothing, evangelistic outreaches to the homeless, etc.; but instead runs for public office or becomes a lobbyist for a certain political cause, it will challenge the very heart of their spirituality—and their leadership's spirituality.

I am by no means encouraging a rebellious or disrespectful attitude toward those God has placed in authority over you. They watch over your soul. Remember this verse from the introduction to this book? It is a key principle of the kingdom of God.

> *Obey them that have the rule over you, and submit yourselves:*
> *for they watch for your souls, as they that must give account,*
> *that they may do it with joy, and not with grief: for that is*
> *unprofitable for you.*
>
> Hebrews 13:17

There is a significant difference between being submissive and being obedient. You can be respectful and submissive to those in authority over you but respectfully disobey them when God is telling you to do something that they believe to be wrong. Just be certain that you have truly heard from God. Sit down and pray and counsel with your leadership before you plunge into something new and different. If your leaders have a serious problem with what you feel called to do, then you need to take that to the Lord and consider what they are saying. After you have exercised all diligence to receive their counsel and wisdom, if you continue to believe that God is calling you to do this, and your elders continue to believe it is wrong, then go ahead without rebellion or disrespect in your heart. In this situation, kingdom work requires you to be disobedient to the expectations of people but obedient to God. However, never are we to harbor rebellion or disrespect in our hearts.

Kingdom ministries or individuals often find themselves moving into places and conditions that others would not dare touch, even taking the chance of being called disobedient for doing so. But when their disobedience is for the sake of making straight a crooked situation and bringing a godly perspective and kingdom principles to bear against an evil system, that disobedience is justified. Justified disobedience will always bring glory to God.

Principle #4
Kingdom Position Often Dictates Kingdom Praise

Why did the Samaritan who was healed of leprosy return to Jesus and glorify God? What made him so fervent and overwhelmed by the touch of the Lord in his life? I believe the answer is found in the fact that Jesus called this man a stranger. The Bible clearly defines "strangers" as Gentiles who didn't know the God of Abraham, Isaac, and Jacob.

> *Wherefore remember, that ye being in time past Gentiles in the flesh, who are called Uncircumcision by that which is called the Circumcision in the flesh made by hands;*
>
> *That at that time ye were without Christ, being aliens from the commonwealth of Israel, and strangers from the covenants of promise, having no hope, and without God in the world:*
>
> Ephesians 2:11,12

Calling the Samaritan a stranger gave two strikes against this man. The first strike was that he had leprosy, which was a disease socially unacceptable, and the second strike was that he was a stranger, an alien, having no hope and without God in the world. The other men had leprosy, but they were Jews who knew God and had a place in His kingdom.

The Samaritan knew that as a Jew, Jesus could have easily ignored him. When Jesus healed his leprosy even though he was a Samaritan, the man was even more grateful. Kingdom passion is intensified when we realize the position that God has delivered us from and the position that God has delivered us to. And when kingdom passion arises, kingdom praise breaks forth.

From this story, we can see that our kingdom position often dictates our kingdom praise. Although the position we find ourselves in today may be painful and difficult, it bears the potential for miracles and revelation to bring us to a new position—and that merits our praise and thanksgiving. Passion for the kingdom of God requires continual growth in faith, maturity, strength, power, compassion, and revelation. Your position today will be the source of tremendous praise tomorrow as you move on in the things of God.

Maybe you are without a church home, a job, a spouse, peace, love, and joy. Right now your position is hard for you. But it is in this position that you are going to realize just what God is able to do. In your present uncomfortable position God can heal you in a way that you never imagined. He can give you a revelation that a book could never teach you. He can sculpture your life so distinctly that nobody can mistake your imprint with someone else's. Where you find yourself at this moment is what God is using to design you like a beautiful, tailor-made suit. Do not despise your position!

Passing from one position to the next brings passion and intensity to our praise. The Samaritan leper returned to praise and thank Jesus because he moved from being just a Samaritan leper to a healed and whole child of God. His praise and thanksgiving to God announced the kingdom of God, the rule of God being manifested in his life. And we are no different. It is our praise that reveals the kingdom of God to those around us, believers and unbelievers alike.

I have learned, in whatsoever state I am, therewith to be content.

Philippians 4:11

The apostle Paul tells us that we must learn to be content no matter what position we are in. We can praise and worship God at all times and in all situations because we know He is delivering us from our present position. Furthermore, we can look back on our previous position and praise Him for it.

What position are you in? What position do you want to be in? By allowing God to pour holiness, miracles, and revelation into your life, you will reach a new position and be miraculously delivered, healed, and set free. You will run to give Him glory. And your kingdom passion will arise and grow in purpose and power.

Ten Essentials for Developing Kingdom Passion

- Develop a deeper understanding of God with the revelation that God is not limited by denominational affiliations but embraces all of His children.

- Identify your gifts, talents, and strengths and apply them where you are. Do not wait for the big opportunities before you get involved.

- Increase your ministry to those who are less fortunate, which keeps you humble and brings you to the next level in the Spirit.

- Be free and focused in your worship experience. Do not put God in a box, and allow the Holy Spirit to minister to you.

- Study materials and produce materials for study that are relevant, informational, and address issues of life from a biblical perspective.

- Find a way to involve people in your program. Everyone has something to contribute to the kingdom of God.

- Do not allow disciplines, by-laws, and procedures to keep your ministry bound. Legalism constrains and inhibits the kingdom of God, which is often revealed in spiritual spontaneity and being free to act when God gives the order to act.

- Reach beyond where you are. The kingdom begins with being captured by evangelism and is revealed when you are caught by mission. Kingdom passion is synonymous with a concern for people's needs and their salvation.

Make Jesus' last commandment (to go and make disciples of all nations) your first priority.

- Do not be afraid to try new approaches to ministry. Be radical, be different, be unprecedented. God is a creator, and He is always revealing new approaches, strategies, and techniques for reaching whom He desires to reach.

- Remember, the kingdom of God is always moving forward, and the worst place in the world to be is where God just left. Do not get stagnant! Pond water that doesn't move eventually smells, and you are called to the fragrance of holiness, miracles, and revelation. You are called to an authentic Pentecostal experience. You are called to be radical!

Part Two

~

THE KINGDOM
PASSION
OF A MAN

8

THE DETOXIFICATION
OF A MAN

Manhood and destiny are determined by decisions. To make godly decisions, decisions that reflect God's will for our lives and that conform us to the image of His Son, we must enter into seasons of purification from time to time. During these times we discover the things that have us intoxicated with anything outside God's kingdom, so we can then break free of them.

Every man who desires to make a contribution to the kingdom of God must experience seasons of detoxification. To speak of detoxification is to confront the reality of being cleansed, purified, and revitalized from within. Detoxification is necessary because while we are meandering our way on this journey from the crib to the grave, there are many proposals, ideas, opportunities, influences, speculations, perspectives, and agendas that affect the way we see the world. The way we see the world then determines how we choose to handle situations that confront us in this life.

Men make decisions based upon their life experiences and education; men who have a passion for the kingdom of God must make decisions based upon the leading of the Holy Spirit and the Word of God. As kingdom men, we must submit ourselves to the cleansing of the Word and the Spirit daily, but then there are those seasons when we must enter a time of intense detoxification from the ungodly influences in our lives.

This intoxication and detoxification notion did not come to me just because I live in a culture where drinking alcohol is common and acceptable. This concept came to me when I began to read about the success and failure of a man by the name of Noah. God spoke to Noah about his call and ordained purpose to assist Him in repopulating the earth. It was also at this time that God reminded Noah that he had dominion over the earth even after the fall of Adam.

> *And God blessed Noah and his sons, and said unto them, Be fruitful, and multiply, and replenish the earth.*
>
> *And the fear of you and the dread of you shall be upon every beast of the earth, and upon every fowl of the air, upon all that moveth upon the earth, and upon all the fishes of the sea; into your hand are they delivered.*

Genesis 9:1,2

Not only did God commission Noah in a similar manner that He had commissioned Adam, but He also established a covenant agreement with Noah, and said in verse 9, "And, I, behold, I establish my covenant with you, and with your seed after you." It was after God established this covenant with Noah that God sealed it by way of a rainbow in the sky.

And the bow shall be in the cloud; and I will look upon it, that I may remember the everlasting covenant between God and every living creature of all flesh that is upon the earth.

And God said unto Noah, This is the token of the covenant, which I have established between me and all flesh that is upon the earth.

Genesis 9:16,17

Noah was on the doorstep of divine paradise. The years of building the ark, enduring the insults and harassments of his neighbors as he preached, and the long days in the ark during the flood were over. All he had to do was to keep the covenant by replenishing the earth. He had everything right there in his hand and nothing about which to complain or worry. Colloquially speaking, he was set for life. Unfortunately, even though Noah had a covenant with Almighty God and had obeyed Him in everything up until now, his flesh got the best of him. He planted a vineyard, partook of the wine it produced, and proceeded to get drunk.

And Noah began to be an husbandman, and he planted a vineyard:

And he drank of the wine, and was drunken; and he was uncovered within his tent.

Genesis 9:20,21

Dr. Charles Gilchrist Adams delivered a sermon on this subject that is a mainstay in many preaching circles. Adams dissected this story and came up with a title for the message that described it best. His subject was "Drunk on the Eve of Reconstruction." In that sermon, Adams tried to convey that while God was preparing Noah to reconstruct creation, replenish the earth, and function under his covenant right, he was found by his sons to be drunk and naked. Noah was intoxicated with something other than the Lord.

Like other men who are intoxicated with anything but the Lord, Noah does not have clear vision and his faculties are hindered. His eyes are swollen and red, and he reeks of alcohol. He is staggering. He has no ability to stand straight and tall as God intended. His judgment, reason, and decision-making are off course. He has no idea what is happening around him or through him. All that God is ready to do with his life is put on hold because Noah's intoxication has put him out of position to be used by God.

What a scenario for us to acknowledge in our modern world today! When we look at the position and status of many men, we see that they are just like Noah. God is ready to use them to replenish the earth with the seed of His Spirit. God is ready to bestow unto them what He has covenanted with them. God is ready to use them to change the course of this world. But sadly enough, too many kingdom men cannot be used for God's glory because, like Noah, they are intoxicated with the wine of the world.

I'm not speaking of drunkenness with the *wine* of the world, but I am speaking of intoxication from the many *proposals, ideas, opportunities, influences, speculations, perspectives, and agendas* that we are confronted with in this life. They intoxicate men to the point where they have no idea that they are naked. In other words, they have staggered away from God and have no clue that they have ceased fellowship with Him. Like Noah, these men become drunk on the things of this world and are rendered useless and senseless.

I have concluded that there are merely three things that keep men of today intoxicated with the wine of the world. Those three things are: Sex, Money, and Power. This is not a new notion. The Bible says it this way:

> *For all that is in the world, the lust of the flesh, and the lust of the eyes, and the pride of life, is not of the Father, but is of the world.*
>
> 1 John 2:16

The lust of the flesh refers to sex, the lust of the eyes refers to money, and the pride of life refers to power. These are the three things that I believe have many men intoxicated—in the Church. When a kingdom man detoxifies himself and cleanses himself from these three things, turning back to his first love, Jesus Christ, and seeking first His kingdom, God can use him mightily for kingdom purposes.

The Intoxication of Sex

It is very obvious that we are living in a sex-crazed society. It seems that in every newspaper or magazine we read, in every television show or movie, in a perfume advertisement on the counter of a department store or a subliminal message in a restaurant, there is an image or a phrase that will cause us to think about sex. Sex is in our music, our classrooms, and our churches. To put it bluntly, sex is everywhere. The problem that we have with the intoxication of sex is that it seems as though many men enjoy the promotion of sex and some are driven by it.

The intoxication of sex can literally destroy a man. We have seen this through all of history. If men do not have discipline in this area of their lives, it will ruin their lives. What would make Amnon sleep with his sister Tamar and destroy his chances to be king of Israel? The intoxication of sex. What would make Samson lay his head in the lap of Delilah and give her the information his enemies needed to capture him? The intoxication of sex. What would make a strong king like David fall, causing him to sleep with another man's wife and then murder a loyal soldier to cover it up? The intoxication of sex. The list goes on, but the reality that I am seeking to convey is that our society—and the church in America—is consumed with sex.

We have allowed God's intention for sex to become perverted and deformed. The reason we have disfigured the original intent of sex is because we have misunderstood its purpose. In many ways sex has been dysfunctionalized by power games in relationships, forms of masturbation, places where exotic dancers will prance on a table top, sex toys available in exotic stores, harassments for job promotions, and images on television and in magazines that portray sex as casual and without commitment. We are intoxicated with sex because we have reduced the act of marital intimacy to an animalistic function where anything goes: fornication, adultery, homosexuality, lesbianism, bisexuality, pedophilia, and the list goes on.

What is the Church's answer? If we are going to ever get delivered from this intoxication, it is essential that we begin to deal with the intoxication with sex in our pulpits, in Bible studies, and in news articles. Leaders must reveal to the people of God the true intents and purposes for sex.

For this cause shall a man leave his father and mother, and shall be joined unto his wife, and they two shall be one flesh.

This is a great mystery: but I speak concerning Christ and the church.

Ephesians 5:31,32

The Bible reveals that experiencing intimacy with your mate is a type of the Bride of Christ's intimacy with Jesus, our Bridegroom. As husband and wife become one in spirit, soul, and body, they get a revelation of what it means to be one with the Lord. Having sex God's way becomes sacred and beautiful as well as pleasurable. Then, out of this sacred union of worship, we accomplish another of God's purposes for sex: procreation.

So God created man in his own image, in the image of God created he him; male and female created he them.

And God blessed them, and God said unto them, Be fruitful, and multiply, and replenish the earth.

Genesis 1:27,28

Procreation is not just having kids. God blesses us and commands us to populate His earth with godly sons and daughters.

He wants children who will love Him, worship Him, and serve Him and Him alone. How many churches have old folks and middle-aged folks who love the Lord, but their children are intoxicated with the world, having sex when they're still babies, having children out of wedlock, and getting AIDS and other sexually transmitted diseases?

If the Church is going to detoxify itself with regard to sex, I believe that detoxification must begin with the men. Women and children will respect and welcome our leadership in this area. They do not mind following husbands and fathers who lead in love, righteousness, and truth. When husbands and fathers purify themselves and keep themselves pure, modeling fidelity and holiness in the home, teaching their families that a loving marriage is the only place God created for sex, their wives and children will have a healthy, godly understanding of sex.

The world's view that causes intoxication with sex has destroyed too many people in the past. Men with a passion for God's kingdom must change this trend by detoxifying their sexual lives. Only then does the Church have a chance to eradicate children having children, the spread of HIV and AIDS, the need to rape, and the treatment of women as biological toys to satisfy our physical urges. Only then can the Church deliver homosexuals and lesbians from the deception of the enemy to see their perversion and understand that the blood of Jesus Christ can set them free from it.

It is time for real kingdom men to take a stand for biblical truth and let the world know that having sex with everyone they meet is nothing to brag about—in this life and certainly not the next. This does not impress God. It is time for real kingdom men to get detoxified by getting the help and counsel they need from their brothers and elders in Christ. It is time for them to throw out pornography, treat women with respect, keep their hearts and minds pure, be loving and wise husbands and fathers, and become role models not only in their homes and churches but in their communities.

Being a godly man, a faithful husband, a wise father, and a productive and respected citizen in church and community is something a man will never need to brag about because everyone else will be bragging on him! I implore you, Sir, to refuse to allow the world's intoxication with sex to destroy your fellowship with God, your family, your future, your calling and profession, your health, your relationships, and the unity and peace in your church. Begin to purify yourself today.

The Intoxication of Money

Recently I watched a television show that has gained great popularity. It is entitled *Lifestyles of the Rich and Famous*. The host of the program took us on a tour of an elaborate and well-decorated home, showing us the hand-made curtains, the plush carpet, a view of the ocean, and thirteen bathrooms that had marble floors. I was stunned for a minute. I was struck with what the world believes it means to be wealthy in a society where only approximately 2 percent can really enjoy that kind of wealth.

This is what Stanley and Danko wrote about in their book *The Millionaire Next Door.* They stated, "It is unfortunate that some people judge others by their choice in foods, beverages, suits, watches, motor vehicles, and such. To them, superior people have excellent taste in consumer goods. But it is easier to purchase products that denote superiority than to be actually superior in economic achievement."

Many people fall into the category of being wealthy because they are able to obtain some very costly things. However, in actuality their portfolio would show that they can't afford them. In our society, wealth is found more in appearances than in reality. If people were to pay all their debts, little or nothing would be left. They have deceived themselves into believing that they are wealthy.

No matter how truthful, too many kingdom men have become intoxicated with money and material things. They justify this by saying that the Bible tells us that God desires for us to walk steadfastly in health and prosperity, using the following verse of scripture again and again.

> *Beloved, I wish above all things that thou mayest prosper and be in health, even as thy soul prospereth.*
>
> 3 John 2

Sir, God wants you to prosper—as your soul prospers. This is the key that we often miss. And the Holy Spirit goes on to explain this in more detail in the verses following.

For I rejoiced greatly, when the brethren came and testified of the truth that is in thee, even as thou walkest in the truth.

I have no greater joy than to hear that my children walk in truth.

3 John 3,4

The kingdom man must walk in truth. The apostle John states emphatically that his greatest joy is to hear that his disciples walk in truth. Why was this his greatest joy? Because when a kingdom man walks in truth, his soul will prosper, and that prospering soul (mind, will, emotions) will cause him to be in health and experience financial blessing. But that is not all. Look at the next verses in this passage of Scripture.

Beloved, thou doest faithfully whatsoever thou doest to the brethren, and to strangers;

Which have borne witness of thy charity before the church: whom if thou bring forward on their journey after a godly sort, thou shalt do well:

Because that for his name's sake they went forth, taking nothing of the Gentiles.

3 John 5-7

When the kingdom man walks in truth, his soul prospers; and when his soul prospers, which could also be defined as kingdom passion, he lives in health and financial prosperity. Then the kingdom man, because he walks in truth and has a passion for the kingdom, uses his health and prosperity to assist the brethren and be a witness of God's love and care to strangers. In 3 John 7 the apostle John commends the believers for taking such good care of these strangers that they didn't need to get anything from unbelievers. The church met all their needs!

Sir, if believers from another town or country walked into your church, would the brothers in your church see that they had a place to stay, good food to eat, and all their needs met while they were in town? If they wanted to do this, would the brothers in your church have the means to provide every need for these strangers passing through?

This account in 3 John is a sharp contrast to what we see in most churches today, and the responsibility lies with the men. The problem that many kingdom men have with money is multifaceted. Many men today

- believe that money is the answer to all problems;

- have developed a love for their money over their family, church, and community;

- have ascribed to a very demeaning and demonic approach to making money, which means that money is now their Lord; and

- derive their personal value and worth from money.

This is not a picture of a passionate kingdom man who walks in truth, seeks first the kingdom, and has a soul that is prospering. Again, I contend that God desires all men to be blessed beyond measure and to prosper in their lifetimes; but if we do not take a moment and understand the proper purpose for money, we will not be effective or fruitful in the kingdom of

God. We will become intoxicated with money, and the intoxication of money will

- make a man kill his parents for his inheritance or his wife for the insurance money,

- make a corporate executive blow a $200,000 a year job for a $15,000.00 embezzlement,

- make a young man sell drugs to his brother and sister even though the drugs are killing them,

- make a husband make his wife sleep with other men to get out of debt,

- make a man with one month left on probation rob a store for $50.00 in the register,

- make the owner of a restaurant chain sell bad products, and

- make a preacher compromise the gospel to raise a good offering.

The biblical and correct attitude toward money is not to love it, to trust in it, or to look to it for any kind of security or well-being, but to see it as a tool God has given to establish His covenant in the earth. Money is a tool. It is not to be worshiped or coveted or esteemed. It is only to be respected and understood for its God-given purpose. This is the truth a kingdom man must walk in to be effective.

The biblical and correct use of money, therefore, is to establish God's covenant in the earth.

But thou shalt remember the Lord thy God: for it is he that giveth thee power to get wealth, that he may establish his covenant which he sware unto thy fathers, as it is this day.

Deuteronomy 8:18

The Intoxication of Power

When we consider the many scandals that are taking place within the business community and political leadership of our nation, scandals that reflect obvious moral decay in our culture, we must admit that there is a serious problem with those who wield power in America. The scandal of the Enron Corporation, that violated the trust of its employees by using the investments of hard workers for illegal gain, was obviously an abuse of power. At the same time, we have been outraged at how many Catholic bishops were having sex with male children in their parishes. These were the little ones whom God had placed in their care, the ones to whom they represented God the Father. Their sin was not only an embarrassment to the Church universal, but yet another obvious abuse of power.

Then there was the scandal in the oval office, occupied by our 42nd President of the United States, Bill Clinton. For years newspapers were filled with articles—not about how well he was running the country—but about his inability to make a sound, moral decision with regard to one of his interns, Monica Lewinsky. President Clinton indiscriminately used the power vested in him by the United States of America for his personal pleasure and gain. He is not the only president who is guilty of this misuse of power, no doubt, but he got caught. Power makes many men so drunk that abuse of their authority becomes a normal way of life. They fail to be governed by that which they confess—even when it is Jesus Christ as their Lord and Savior.

My definition of power is an individual or a group having the influence to achieve their expected goal or purpose. Oftentimes, if a goal or a purpose is not agreeable to an individual or group, the leader or leaders will abuse their power to alter the goal or purpose to accommodate their own personal, selfish agenda. Therefore, if power is not put in its correct context and understood to be used for the influence of positive good, men will continue to be intoxicated with it and become ineffective in the kingdom of God. For example, many churches today are experiencing spiritual confusion because men of the church are vying for control. They have lost sight of the goal and purpose because they are intoxicated with personal power.

We have aborted God's divine blueprint for power in the Church and in society as a whole. We have decided that the system needs to be centered around who has power and control, but God has charged those in leadership to be servants. In Matthew 20:27-28 Jesus commanded, "And whosoever will be chief among you, let him be your servant: Even as the Son of man came not to be ministered unto, but to minister, and to give his life a ransom for many." In this text Jesus explicitly illustrates the need for those in positions of power and leadership to focus on those they are serving by living according to this mandate of God.

Being in leadership involves the transfer and acquisition of power. The problem with deciding who is going to have power or be in leadership is that this 1) denies the plan of God, 2) detracts from the presence of God, and 3) reduces the deity of God. The Church is not about power and control, but it is about submitting fully to the Holy Spirit and the plan that God has for His church.

This is the argument that Bill Hull in his book, 7 *Steps to Transform Your Church,* tried to make when he said, "The purpose of authority is to influence human behavior and provide behavioral parameters."[2] In the New Testament, the Greek word *exousia* is translated authority and power, denoting freedom of action with authority that is delegated.[3] Authority also means power. Scripture teaches that we have this kind of spiritual power available through the Holy Spirit, who empowers God's people to meaningful action. Leaders empowered by the Holy Spirit provide accountability in exhortation, encouragement, and correction. They give vision, strategy, and shape to mission. If leaders will lead correctly (1 Peter 5:1-6) and the congregation ministers properly (Heb. 13:17), the body will mature exponentially (Eph. 4:16-17).

This is the proper use of power and authority in the Church. Notice that it in no way leads to *who* is in control, but power is used for kingdom enhancement. If the Church can ever get the function of power right, I believe that this will spread to men in the larger society, help men to understand

- what it means to be the head of the home,

- why God gave them more physical strength than women,

- how to operate in a godly manner in high levels of influence,

- never to take advantage of someone who has less influence, and

- how to avoid abusing their power for their own gain mentally, emotionally, physically, and financially.

If you are going to be a kingdom man, you must know the proper use of power and begin to make a difference in your community because of it. For example, our church is planning a conference designed to minister salvation to drug dealers in the Winston-Salem community. It was imperative for me to consider the power that these individuals have in the community and try to channel them in the right direction.

Individually and collectively this particular sector of society has the ability to convince young boys to distribute poison to their neighbors and family members; they have the business savvy to orchestrate a plan of action that earns them profit without waiting for a paycheck and without giving the government a portion of their income; and they have the ingenuity to make this lifestyle appear glamorous in order to draw others to the use and sale of drugs.

Because so many young boys are in dire need of mentoring, these men take advantage of that need and blatantly misuse their power to lead young boys down a path of destruction instead of steering them toward education. They use their ability to profit from an illegal substance, when they should use this power to create and implement businesses that have a positive impact on the community. This would ensure their own longevity, retirement, and freedom. Moreover, because God desires for the man to be the head of the household, the ex-drug dealer who is a Christian can draw young men away from the streets to a life with Jesus Christ, where the supply of love and affirmation and security is endless and the benefits far outweigh the risks.

With these things in mind, our church seeks to properly direct the power of the drug traffickers by providing a seminar for them. We must help them understand the importance of community empowerment, assist them in understanding the violation of community through criminal acts, and illustrate for them the effects negative music and other subliminal influences have on their lives, articulating vile forms of interaction. In this conference there will be testimonies of former drug dealers, a job fair that connects them with legal work, and most importantly, preaching to lead them to Jesus Christ. It is our hope that through this conference deliverance will go forth and they will understand the proper use of power.

God's Detoxification Program

Because we are living in a culture where we are intoxicated with sex, money, and power, a kingdom man must go through detoxification to be effective. The primary way of detoxification is the process of purifying ourselves and lining ourselves up by renewing our minds with God's Word and obeying the teaching and leading of the Holy Spirit.

I beseech you therefore, brethren, by the mercies of God, that ye present your bodies a living sacrifice, holy, acceptable unto God, which is your reasonable service.

And be not conformed to this world: but be ye transformed by the renewing of your mind, that ye may prove what is that good, and acceptable, and perfect, will of God.

Romans 12:1,2

Being transformed by the Word and the Spirit detoxifies your heart and mind. The apostle Paul could have written, "Be detoxified by the renewing of your mind." Then you will possess the proper attitude and exhibit the godly behavior to effect kingdom change in a lost world. In the words of verse 2 above, you will prove or live by example the good, acceptable, and perfect will of God. God's will is always good, acceptable, and perfect. And the detoxified kingdom man seeks, hears, and obeys the will of God.

Secondly, we purify ourselves and line ourselves up with God's kingdom purposes and plans in our relationships with others, believers and unbelievers. We have to live what we believe in our marriage, in our families, in our churches, at our workplace, and in our communities. No man can detox himself and maintain passion for God's kingdom by himself. The world realizes this truth, that no man is an island unto himself, which is why there are support groups in every community for just about any problem a human being is facing.

Listed below are two detoxification programs. In the first column I paraphrase the twelve steps that alcoholics go through in their process of detoxification. In the second column I have listed the steps in a program designed for men who are seeking to detoxify from the world and establish passion for God's kingdom. Although both programs are based upon scriptural principles, they have some striking differences.

Read and become a Kingdom Man!

12 Step Detoxification Program for an Alcoholic[4]	*12 Step Detoxification Program for a Kingdom Man*
Confess to be powerless over alcohol and that your life is unmanageable.	Confess you are powerless over sin and your life is unmanageable without Jesus Christ in your life.
Confess that there is a power greater than yourself that can restore sanity.	Confess that only Jesus Christ can give you peace and sustain you from being intoxicated with power, money, and sex.
Make a decision to turn your will and life over to God as you understand Him.	Make a decision to surrender everything to God, and let God begin to direct your path and every move of your life.
Do a searching and fearless inventory of yourself.	

Admit to God, yourself, and another human being the exact nature of your wrongdoing.

Do a searching and fearless inventory of yourself, knowing that God has already forgiven you for anything that you might find.

Admit to God, yourself, and another believer where you have faltered, and then set your eyes on new sights and higher heights.

Be ready to have God reveal defects of character.

Study God's Word to find out your true image and definition, the person God made you to be.

Ask God to remove your shortcomings.

Ask God to help you to use your past shortcomings as a testimony and a point of ministry, and tell others that if God did it for you, He can do it for them.

Make a list of all persons you harmed and be willing to make amends.

Make a list of all persons who have harmed you, let them know you have forgiven them, and move forward with your life.

Make direct amends to such people whenever possible, except when doing so would injure them and others.

Make amends to people you have harmed and ask for their forgiveness.

Continue to take personal inventory and admit when you are wrong.

Make a list of goals and projections that you want to accomplish in your life, and never be afraid to start over if you make a mistake.

Through prayer and meditation continue to improve your contact with God.

Once you confess your new life, become a part of some ministry that will keep you covered in prayer and meditation. Find a ministry you feel called to and work for the Lord.

Having completed these steps, take this message to alcoholics and practice these principles in all affairs.

Having accepted Jesus Christ as Lord of your life, do not be afraid to evangelize and minister Christ wherever you go. There are other men who need to be detoxed.

While I consider the **12 Step Detoxification Program for a Kingdom Man** a very comprehensive way for all men to become effective, it is important to continue reading! Each chapter will help you to further develop your emancipation and your deliverance from the intoxication of the things in this world.

9

THE DELIVERANCE OF A KINGDOM MAN

When a man is born again, he is delivered out of the kingdom of darkness, out from the world system, and out from under the rule of the devil. He is delivered into the kingdom of light, the plans and purposes of God, and now serves under the King of kings, Jesus Christ. This is the most important deliverance a man can experience in life, but being born again is not the end of deliverance. Whether we're five or fifty-five when we are born again, we are spiritual babes who need to grow up in the kingdom of God.

> That we henceforth be no more children, tossed to and fro, and carried about with every wind of doctrine, by the sleight of men, and cunning craftiness, whereby they lie in wait to deceive;
>
> But speaking the truth in love, may grow up into him in all things, which is the head, even Christ.
>
> Ephesians 4:14,15

We are called to become like Jesus, to "grow up into Him in all things," and that is a monumental, seemingly impossible calling. That's why there is no greater celebration in the body of Christ than when a man of the kingdom experiences a real deliverance in his life. Every kingdom man who is effective and growing into the image of Jesus can give his personal history of deliverance. And yet, there is nothing more misunderstood in the body of Christ today than deliverance!

Deliverance happens when something on the inside of you changes, and you never see life the same again. Deliverance is the release of something demonic, worldly, and carnal that has held you back from being all God wants you to be and fulfilling all He's called you to do. Deliverance can be achieved in the quiet realization that you have believed a lie or through a more spectacular release from demonic oppression when another believer prays for you.

The Bible clearly tells us how deliverance happens: by knowing the truth and embracing the truth, which shatters all lies and deception of the enemy, exposing his evil schemes and demonic strongholds in your life. Then the bondage you walked in falls away. Whether this happens immediately or over time, you get delivered. You are free.

> Then said Jesus to those Jews which believed on him, If ye continue in my word, then are ye my disciples indeed;
>
> And ye shall know the truth, and the truth shall make you free.
>
> John 8:31,32

There is nothing more admirable than a delivered kingdom man. He is free because he walks in the Spirit and in Truth. Only as free men of God can we move from where we are to where God desires us to be. And we position ourselves for deliverance when we make the decision to change and declare that things must change—not tomorrow, not later, but now.

It reminds me of a story that one of my former barbers used to tell. One night, after a long week of cutting hair, he decided to go to a place where they sold liquor by the drink. When he walked in, he sat beside a woman who was obviously there for the same reason. Within minutes, a man he did not know came in and put a gun to his head! The gunman had mistaken the barber for someone else, but there was no time to discuss this or to try to persuade the gunman that he had the wrong man.

People began screaming and rushing to safety, and the gunman stood there, pressing the gun against the barber's head and yelling, "It's over! It's over for you!" The barber was sure that his life was about to end, but when the gunman was about to pull the trigger, the clip fell out of the gun. Bullets scattered over the floor, and I can hear my former barber say, "When the bullets hit the floor, I hit the back door, and I have been running for the Lord ever since!" He made the decision that some things in his life needed to change right then!

This was his story of deliverance. What is yours? In order for you to be a kingdom man who wins other men to the kingdom, it is important for you to have a story about the changes that God has made in your life. Many men think that their story of deliverance has to be grand or spectacular as my former barber's was. What makes a deliverance story meaningful is not why or how it happened but that it did happen. Changes on the inside cause everything to change on the outside. The amount of truth you walk in determines the degree to which the kingdom of God is evidenced in your life. These changes can happen in a twinkling of an eye or they can happen over a period of years.

Someone may say, "Well, my life changed by just simply listening to a sermon. I heard the truth like I never heard it before and knew that that was my day to be set free. I went to the altar, a brother began to pray for me, and I felt a huge weight lift off of me. From that day, I haven't had to have a drink."

Someone else may say, "It didn't happen for me all at once, but it was a gradual process. As a matter of fact, I can't recall the date or time. All I know is that after five years of going to church, doing the detox program, and praying and reading God's Word and seeking God for everything, I don't have the desire to drink, smoke, or do drugs anymore. In fact, I can't remember the last time I did any of that. A change has been made in my life."

There are some who can remember the very day and hour when the Holy Spirit liberated their soul from hell's chains; while others just realize one day that they have been miraculously changed by the grace of God. But I can promise you one thing. The delivered kingdom man doesn't care how it happened or how long it took. He's just glad he's delivered!

Deliverance Happens at Midnight

Much of the writing in the book of Acts has been attributed to Luke, a physician and a writer who gave great attention to detail. With that in mind, it is interesting that in Acts 16 Luke records that Paul and Silas, who had been beaten and thrown in jail, prayed and sang praises to God at *midnight*.

Midnight is the darkest time of the night. It is the pinnacle of darkness, representing the crescendo of a dismal moment. There are physical midnights when the stars hang in their sockets and the moon shines as a lantern from eternity. But there are also spiritual midnights. A spiritual midnight constitutes anything that keeps you from moving forward in God or knowing God more intimately. Here are some examples of spiritual midnights.

- Your criminal record makes you feel inferior and you can't seem to function as a whole man or pursue the dream job you desire.

- Options are limited and you feel trapped because of your socio-economic status, family history, work record, societal pressures, or racial prejudice.

- You catch your spouse in a relationship with another man.

- Your children have not forgiven you for divorcing their mother.

- The child support is due but you have no money to pay it.

- The lack of your father's attention when you were growing up is now hindering you from showing love to your own children.

- You children are in trouble with sex, drugs, or the law.

- You are addicted to pornography.

- You are obese and your weight is life threatening.

- You are making legal, moral, or ethical compromises to be promoted on the job and to make more money.

- Alcohol and drugs have become an addictive behavior for your life.

When your purpose is in question, your place is undefined, you just don't fit in anywhere, or you are clinging to a thin hope—that is spiritual midnight. While midnight is the darkest time of the night, technically midnight only lasts for a fraction of a second. At 12:00:01 morning begins, and it is the start of a new day. Therefore, if you can just endure this fraction of darkness in your life, you will experience morning.

> *Weeping may endure for a night, but joy cometh in the morning.*
> Psalm 30:5

In truth, spiritual midnight is good news. It means that God is about to deliver you. You are on the verge of revelation and elevation! All you need is to hold fast to the Word and the Spirit and have faith that the morning is coming.

One of the most powerful illustrations of Christian faith is unequivocally demonstrated by Paul and Silas in the Philippian jailhouse. They lived a story of deliverance at the midnight hour, and we see that when they got delivered, so did many others. Your deliverance will change your life so deeply that it will have a ripple effect of change on everyone in your life. This is bringing the kingdom of God into the earth. Paul and Silas's story exemplifies this truth.

> *And it came to pass, as we went to prayer, a certain damsel possessed with a spirit of divination met us, which brought her masters much gain by soothsaying:*
>
> *The same followed Paul and us, and cried, saying, These men are the servants of the most high God, which show unto us the way of salvation.*
>
> *And this did she many days. But Paul, being grieved, turned and said to the spirit, I command thee in the name of Jesus Christ to come out of her. And he came out the same hour.*
>
> Acts 16:16-18

Circumstances always get much, much worse before deliverance happens. The men who were using this girl's "gift" of divination to make money were enraged when Paul delivered her. They brought Paul and Silas to the town magistrates, told the whole town that Paul and Silas were causing nothing but trouble, and incited the people to beat them.

> *And the multitude rose up together against them [Paul and Silas]: and the magistrates rent off their clothes, and commanded to beat them.*
>
> *And when they had laid many stripes upon them, they cast them into prison, charging the jailor to keep them safely:*

Who, having received such a charge, thrust them into the inner prison, and made their feet fast in the stocks.

Acts 16:22-24 [insert mine]

After being beaten, Paul and Silas sat in chains and shackles with cuts and bruises on their backs. But instead of having a pity party, at midnight they began to pray and sing songs. It was when they worshiped God in their terrible condition that the earth began to shake in such fashion that it shook the prison doors open.

And at midnight Paul and Silas prayed, and sang praises unto God: and the prisoners heard them.

And suddenly there was a great earthquake, so that the foundations of the prison were shaken: and immediately all the doors were opened, and every one's bands were loosed.

Acts 16:25,26

When they were subjected to injustice and brutality, Paul and Silas refused to incorporate that same anger in their spirits. Rather than walking in the rage that was so vehemently directed toward them, they took a different approach. They retreated into the Spirit and the Truth, and they began to pray and sing songs of praise.

When situations in your life are not right, do you run to God?

When things in your life are so low, do you commune with the Most High?

When it seems like your world is crashing, do you enter into that sacred place of inner peace?

When there is no exit from chaos, conflict, and confusion, do you seek the serenity of His presence?

What do you do in the midnights of your life?

When Paul and Silas entered a midnight of their lives, when they needed deliverance, the first thing they did was start praying. They took their troubles right to God.

Prayer Is Not for Wimps

Too often men bring their frustrations and their disappointments of life to people and places that can't provide a way of deliverance for them. They turn to cursing, drinking, drugs, pornography, hot-rod cars, or sexual promiscuity to escape their frustrations and disappointments. Although these things may help them to feel better for awhile, none of them will set them free. These escapes provide a temporary relief, but in the long run they cause the midnight to grow even darker.

Paul and Silas knew that deliverance could only be found in God, and so they began to pray. Prayer will sustain you through the difficult situation and beyond it. Prayer gives you a relief that is long lasting. Prayer is essential in a midnight situation because it brings a benediction to trials, temptations, and trouble. Prayer moves us from solo to symphony with God and His heavenly host. As a wise cleric once said, "Prayer is not that which gets our will done in heaven, but it gets God's will done on earth. Prayer is the key to morning, and the lightning bolt of the night. And if anybody is a stranger to prayer, they are a stranger to power."

What is the midnight you are facing right now? Do your children need deliverance from the hand of the enemy? Does your family need deliverance from poverty and lack? Do you or does someone you love need deliverance from a sickness or a disease? The power to walk through your midnight and get victory through it and over it is found first of all in prayer.

The power of God rises up in us and comes upon us when we pray. James 1:5 tells us that if we lack wisdom, if we need answers, then we should ask God. He will never put us down, but He will tell us everything we need to know and put our hearts at ease. Prayer is one of the most important keys to being a passionate kingdom man.

Pray without ceasing.

1 Thessalonians 5:17

I will therefore that men pray every where, lifting up holy hands, without wrath and doubting.

1 Timothy 2:8

Is any among you afflicted? let him pray. Is any merry? let him sing psalms.

James 5:13

Never forget to pray—whether you're in a midnight hour or a sunshine hour. Learn to turn to prayer instead of those things that cause destruction and ultimately make your night darker. A kingdom man must understand that prayer is no sign of weakness; prayer is one of his greatest strengths. Prayer is not just something that the ladies of the church do!

For too long men of the Church have abdicated this most important responsibility. It is not just the woman's job to pray for the home, children, church, or any other need. It is the man's job to pray. Pray without ceasing, and never cease to pray. Sir, it takes a real kingdom man to pray!

Praise and Worship

Paul and Silas also sang songs of praise and worship to God during their midnight. What prompted them to sing? Perhaps they knew the power of praise and worship from studying the Old Testament. In the Old Testament praises to God were sung by Israelites to defeat their enemies in battle. One of the most famous examples is when King Johashaphat was facing a formidable enemy and sent forth the praise team in front of his army.

> And they rose early in the morning, and went forth into the wilderness of Tekoa: and as they went forth, Jehoshaphat . . . appointed singers unto the Lord, and that should praise the beauty of holiness, as they went out before the army, and to say, Praise the Lord; for his mercy endureth for ever.
>
> And when they began to sing and to praise, the Lord set ambushments against the children of Ammon, Moab, and mount Seir, which were come against Judah; and they were smitten.
>
> 2 Chronicles 20:20-22

Certainly Paul and Silas knew this story well when they began singing in their distress. They also knew how music was used to mellow the heart of the enemy and drive away evil spirits. When Saul was the king of Israel, he became depressed and demonized because he had disobeyed God. He sent for a young shepherd boy named David because David's anointed music soothed his soul.

> *And it came to pass, when the evil spirit from God was upon Saul, that David took an harp, and played with his hand: so Saul was refreshed, and was well, and the evil spirit departed from him.*
>
> 1 Samuel 16:23

From these two biblical examples, we see the tremendous delivering power of praise and worship to God. If kingdom men get a revelation of this truth, they can get free and stay free. Sir, it is time to open your mouth and sing praises to your God!

One of the most challenging ministries in my church is the male chorus. I have often wondered why it is so difficult to gather men together, stand them up in a choir, and get them to sing. Then it occurred to me that many men won't join the choir because they believe that they must master singing. It is good to have a voice as smooth as silk, but singing is more of a soul connection. Singing is the soul giving definition to a situation. Singing is the collaboration of the voice and an expectation. Singing is the acknowledgment of your past, present, and future. And when your soul connects with the right song, the song can reveal answers to your questions and solutions to your problems. The song of praise brings you to the place of deliverance.

Paul and Silas began singing songs of praise, and those songs carried the same power as the songs David and Jehoshaphat sang in the Old Testament. Just as a song mellowed the heart of Saul and ambushed the enemy of Jehoshaphat, the praises of Paul and Silas brought an earthquake, unlocked their shackles, and opened the prison doors.

Praise God when times are good and praise Him when times are not so good. If you want God to deliver you from whatever is holding you back, you must praise Him with all your heart, soul, mind, and strength. In fact, there is no more macho picture of a man than one who passionately and consistently praises God at all times and in all situations.

Your Midnight Can Lead to Somebody Else's Daylight

When the jailer awoke in the earthquake and saw that the prison doors were opened, he pulled out his sword to kill himself. In those days it was the ultimate failure and disgrace for a jailer to lose a prisoner. But Paul stopped singing and called out to him not to kill himself, putting his heart at rest by telling him that the prisoners were still there.

> *And the keeper of the prison awaking out of his sleep, and seeing the prison doors open, he drew out his sword, and would have killed himself, supposing that the prisoners had been fled.*
>
> *But Paul cried with a loud voice, saying, Do thyself no harm: for we are all here.*
>
> Acts 16:27,28

Have you ever wondered why Paul and Silas didn't bolt right out the door the moment they were set free? They had been in prayer and worship, and they knew that God was going to do something magnificent and miraculous that night. It wasn't just an earthquake or the prison doors flying open. In the midst of their midnight, God was going to save someone!

> *Then he called for a light, and sprang in, and came trembling, and fell down before Paul and Silas,*
>
> *And brought them out, and said, Sirs, what must I do to be saved?*
>
> Acts 16:29,30

In the midnight hour of deliverance, not only is morning coming for you, but your midnight can lead others to their daylight. That's exactly what happened in the case of Paul and Silas. Their singing and praying led the jailer right to the Morning Star. As a result of their faith and trust in God, the jailer who was charged to watch them got saved, and then his whole household got saved.

> *And they said, Believe on the Lord Jesus Christ, and thou shalt be saved, and thy house.*
>
> *And they spake unto him the word of the Lord, and to all that were in his house.*
>
> *And he took them the same hour of the night, and washed their stripes; and was baptized, he and all his, straightway.*
>
> *And when he had brought them into his house, he set meat before them, and rejoiced, believing in God with all his house.*
>
> Acts 16:31-34

Paul and Silas made such an impression on the jailer that he fell at their feet and got saved. Then he personally took them out of prison to his home. His family got saved and baptized, and then they all sat down to eat together. Never forget that what you do in your time of midnight will affect the way others around you see and understand God. That's why it is so important for you to share your testimony of deliverance with other men. Let them know what God has demonstrated in your life.

Who can better minister to a man with low-self esteem than a man who has been delivered from low self-esteem? Who can better minister to a young man about the life of a thug or a gangster than a delivered gang member? Who can better lead a cocaine or crack addict to Jesus Christ than a man who has been delivered from that lifestyle? It is important that you understand that when you get delivered, the delivering hand of God keeps on moving in the lives of everyone in your life.

What do you do when you find yourself in a spiritual midnight?

- Don't turn to old bad habits or people who will bring you down—Pray!
  Turn to God, His Word, and the Holy Spirit.

- Don't complain—Exclaim!
  Sing praises to your Deliverer.

- Don't turn away a true friend who is willing to stand with you.
  Embrace the ministry of delivered kingdom men.

- Remember that people care more about you than you think they care.

- Never forget— Deliverance happens in mysterious ways and great men are humble.
  Superman changed his clothes in a phone booth!

Every man's deliverance is a great testimony to other men, and no man's story is any more or any less important than yours. Don't ever think that what God has done in your life is not that important to others. Your testimony might be the only story that can lead someone to Jesus Christ. Your story might be the key that can unlock someone's hardened, hopeless heart to the Holy Spirit's healing touch. Your declaration of how God delivered you at midnight can bring so many others into the dawn of a new day in their lives. Never hesitate to tell your story when God opens the door for you to tell it!

10

THE DEFINED KINGDOM MAN

In order to discuss the true essence of what it means to be a man with passion for the kingdom, it is essential that one understands the power of definition. Definition is simply that which brings clarity to a person or issue for the fruition of its purpose. Definition is making the obscure more profound and bringing light to detail that otherwise could not be seen. A man maintains his passion for God's kingdom when he has spiritual definition. In simple terms, spiritual definition is being defined by God.

One of my favorite illustrations of spiritual definition in the natural is weight lifting, which is something many men pursue but for various reasons. If a man desires definition for his muscles, he will lift less weight and do more repetitions. With less weight and more repetitions, he will begin to see the muscular cuts in the triceps and biceps, and the definition of the physical body comes to fruition. God always uses the physical truths of His creation to demonstrate spiritual truths.

If a man wants to increase his spiritual definition, he must do as the Word of God instructs and pray without ceasing. Prayer is the direct link to God that not only allows us to communicate with Him but also allows Him to feed our spirits. A kingdom man also builds his spiritual definition through studying the Word of God. To be transformed by the renewing of our minds as prescribed in Romans 12:2, it is imperative for us to daily commune with the Lord through the reading of His Word.

I believe most men in the kingdom of God lack spiritual definition. This is why so many Christian men today feel void of purpose, are in the wrong place at the wrong time, and have their priorities out of order. It is spiritual definition that points a man to his calling and destiny and challenges him to live up to what the Bible has pronounced him to be. No man of the kingdom can function without spiritual definition—even Jesus.

Jesus Was Defined

Now when all the people were baptized, it came to pass, that Jesus also being baptized, and praying, the heaven was opened,

And the Holy Ghost descended in a bodily shape like a dove upon him, and a voice came from heaven, which said, Thou art my beloved Son; in thee I am well pleased.

Luke 3:21,22

In this passage in Luke, the heavenly Father pronounces definition of His Son. Up until this moment in time, Jesus walked among the people in obscurity. In other words, there was a time when people did not know that Jesus was the Messiah. I believe it is important to note that obscurity often precedes purpose. Are you in a position right now where people don't know your name? Are they unaware of the gifts, talents, and attributes you bring to the table? Know that it is just a matter of time before God pulls the curtain up and reveals who you are and what you are called to do in the kingdom.

Before His baptism in Luke, Jesus was considered an ordinary man. As a matter of fact, Jesus was standing in line to be baptized by John just like all the others. It was during this ordinary baptism that the heavens opened and a voice cracked the sky to declare, "Thou art my beloved Son; in thee I am well pleased" (Luke 3:22). While Jesus was being publicly affirmed in His calling and destiny by His Father, all of John's followers received definition of Jesus' personhood.

It is important to note that Jesus received definition from His Father. I had two parents in my life until the death of my father in 1982. While I will always cherish the principles my mother shared to help shape my life, it seems that much of the security I developed came because I was fortunate enough to receive definition from my father. It was my father who modeled what it meant to function as a kingdom man. As a pastor who counsels many young people, I have discovered that the reason many turn to destructive lifestyles such as drugs, alcohol, sexual promiscuity, and destructive forms of music is because they are searching for definition from a father.

Again, this is not to underestimate the ability of a mother to raise a son, but a natural father or spiritual father provides a certain kind of stability and confidence, introducing a son to formative principles that will guide him throughout life. I have been fortunate enough to have a godson by the name of Jeremiah, who right now is six years of age. One day while he was getting dressed for school, Jeremiah said to his father, "Daddy, I need you to pray with me."

Jeremiah's father responded by saying, "What is it that you would like me to pray with you about?"

Jeremiah responded, "Daddy, when it's time for us to die, I want you to ask God to please let me and you die together because I am afraid to be here without you being here too."

If that doesn't grip your soul, I don't know what will! Jeremiah was essentially saying, "Daddy, you define my life in such a way that I am afraid that if you die before me, I run the risk of losing my definition." What Jeremiah didn't understand was that definition is about character. Even if his father is not with him one day, the time his father will have spent shaping his belief system, imparting God's wisdom, and impacting his decision-making will give him definition for the rest of his life.

Kingdom men should live their lives in a way that brings definition, clarity, purpose, and meaning to other believers' lives. Kingdom men have the God-given authority to define things and to call things into being. Like Adam, who named every creature on earth, men with a passion for the kingdom of God define those people God brings to them. Sir, it is your responsibility to give spiritual definition to your wife, to your sons and daughters, and to any other human being God brings into your life. If a young man comes to you for counsel or prayer, boldly tell him that God made him a genius, an entrepreneur, a conqueror, the head and not the tail, above and not beneath. You have that authority, and you should never withhold the blessing of spiritual definition.

The Bible tells us to be imitators of God, so we must consider what God pronounced over His Son, Jesus Christ, and do likewise. We must tell our wives and children how much we love them and appreciate the tremendous gifts and abilities God has placed in them. We must nurture and encourage them to stir up their gifts and grow in God. And we must go out of our way to pronounce definition on those who have no one else to do that for them.

A vocal pronouncement is not the only way we receive spiritual definition, however. Although the Father declared that Jesus was His Son in whom He was well pleased, Jesus the Messiah had been defined for centuries in the Holy Scriptures. Throughout the Old Testament the life and purpose of the Messiah to come was prophesied and described in detail in many passages of Scripture. Here are two from the book of Isaiah.

> *Therefore the Lord himself shall give you a sign; Behold, a virgin shall conceive, and bear a son, and shall call his name Immanuel.*
>
> Isaiah 7:14

> *For unto us a child is born, unto us a son is given: and the government shall be upon his shoulder: and his name shall be*

called Wonderful, Counsellor, The mighty God, The everlasting Father, The Prince of Peace.

Of the increase of his government and peace there shall be no end, upon the throne of David, and upon his kingdom, to order it, and to establish it with judgment and with justice from henceforth even for ever. The zeal of the Lord of hosts will perform this.

Isaiah 9:6,7

Just as Jesus was defined by the Word of God, so are we. If a kingdom man never received spiritual definition from his natural father or a spiritual father, he could still receive it from his heavenly Father through the Word of God and the Spirit of God. For example, consider the following passage of Scripture, which gives believers spiritual definition and reveals who they are in Christ.

He hath chosen us in him before the foundation of the world, that we should be holy and without blame before him in love:

Having predestinated us unto the adoption of children by Jesus Christ to himself, according to the good pleasure of his will,

To the praise of the glory of his grace, wherein he hath made us accepted in the beloved.

In whom we have redemption through his blood, the forgiveness of sins, according to the riches of his grace.

Ephesians 1:4-7

This particular passage of Scripture tells us who we are in Christ. We are chosen in Him. We are holy and without blame in Him. He has predestinated us and adopted us. We are fully accepted by Him and beloved. We are redeemed from sin and forgiven of all our sins through the shed blood of Jesus Christ. These verses alone should set a kingdom man's heart on fire!

Overall, I believe the Word of God indicates that there are three major aspects to the spiritual definition of a kingdom man. A man with a passion for God's kingdom will fulfill the roles of priest, prophet, and propitiator.

The Kingdom Man Defined as a Priest

In the Old Testament a priest was one who was set aside to lead the people of God in worship, prayers, thanksgiving, and sacrifices to God. The first time a priest unto God is mentioned is in Genesis 14:18. "And Melchizedek king of Salem brought forth bread and wine: and he was the priest of the most high God."

Later in the Old Testament, God instituted the Levitical priesthood to serve Him in the Tabernacle and then the Temple of Israel. In this priestly order, God ordained a high priest, the only one to enter the Holy of Holies where the Ark of the Covenant and the presence of God dwelt. The high priest was also the mediator between God and His people.

In the New Testament, the book of Hebrews explains that Jesus has now become our high priest, and that He is our high priest forever.

Wherefore in all things it behoved him [Jesus] to be made like unto his brethren, that he might be a merciful and faithful high priest in things pertaining to God, to make reconciliation for the sins of the people.

Hebrews 2:17 [insert mine]

Whither the forerunner is for us entered, even Jesus, made an high priest for ever after the order of Melchisedec.

Hebrews 6:20

Jesus is our high priest and our example. As priests unto God, we must follow Him. This is an essential part of spiritual definition for any man seeking and maintaining passion for God's kingdom. Priestly function for the kingdom man begins with being a follower of Christ. Above all else, he must have a vibrant, daily fellowship with God and His Word. The kingdom man has no passion to impart and nothing to lead his family and others to if he himself doesn't first have intimacy with the Lord.

The kingdom man who receives daily spiritual definition from the Word and the Spirit will also rise up in his spiritual authority, becoming the spiritual head of the home and a godly example in his church, at work, and in his community. As priest, he takes an aggressive approach to leading others to God and discipling those under his care.

Some men will not lead in any capacity of priestly function because they feel that submission to God is feminine, weak, and not something real men do. But worshiping God and leading others into worship has nothing to do with gender. Worship has to do with seeing God for who God is and worshiping Him for who He is.

Jesus led by example and we as priests must lead by example. It is a mockery for a man to encourage his family to go to church if he won't attend himself. It is impossible to lead your family and friends in prayer or encourage them to pray when you are not praying yourself. It is impossible to get your children to study and meditate on God's Word when you never crack the Bible at home. It is impossible to preach and teach the necessity of investing and saving for tomorrow when you spend every dime you get your hands on. It is impossible to expect your wife and children to follow the Lord when you do not follow Him.

The priestly example is a man who strives to live a holy, righteous, compassionate life before his wife and children, his church, his coworkers, and his community. As I have studied the kingdom man's role of priest, I have found eight important aspects of priesthood.

- A priest understands salvation through Jesus Christ and helps others to find God for themselves.

- A priest makes worship in spirit and in truth a priority in his life.

- A priest prays without ceasing and is continuously communicating with God but also has a daily time devoted just to prayer.

- A priest is not afraid to intercede, stand in the gap, and enter into spiritual warfare on behalf of others.

- A priest develops his ability to preach, teach, sing, exhort, and any gifts that God has given him for edification of the body.

- A priest will sacrifice his time, talent, and treasure to establish God's kingdom and assist God's people.

- A priest gives spiritual definition to his wife, his children, and any other human being God sends to him.

- A priest is a leader. Leading is not dominating and conforming everyone to your idea of what a believer should be. Leading is bringing and pointing everyone around you to Jesus, to His Word, to His Spirit.

As a priest under our high priest, Jesus Christ, we are called to encourage and to bring stability to people in all kinds of circumstances and situations. The greatest reward a kingdom man can receive is to see his family and other people in his life living for the Lord because of his influence and assistance. This will bring you more joy, peace, and fulfillment than anything else in life.

The Kingdom Man Defined as a Prophet

This word "prophet" is controversial today, primarily because many people confuse "prophesying" with being a "prophet." To prophesy is to speak divine revelations of God for the purpose of edifying the body of Christ or as a sign to bring an unbeliever to salvation. One believer may prophesy to another believer, giving instruction or encouragement. Or a believer could prophesy to an unbeliever as part of God's plan to lead that individual to the Lord.

However, God calls some men and women to stand in the office of a prophet, which is very different. A prophet declares God's Word and will in unique circumstances. God uses prophets to insure that His Word and will prevail in situations, in churches, and in nations. This is consistent with the Hebrew definition of a prophet, which is derived from the word *nabi,* which means "to bubble forth" or "announce" or "pour forth" the Word of God.[1] In the Greek, the word translated "prophet" is *prophetes,* which means "to tell beforehand...also an interpreter."[2]

There are many characteristics of prophets in the Old Testament, who spoke as the Holy Spirit directed them. They were historians, preachers of religious patriotism, preachers of morality and spirituality. Sometimes they held a pastoral office. They were politicians who stood for God. They were teachers of morality and truth and revelators of God's Word. The common denominator in all of these functions is truth. A prophet cannot be effective if he is not undergirded with truth.

Blaise Pascal once stated, "Unless we know the truth we cannot know it."[3] And Cicero declared, "Our minds possess by nature an insatiable desire to know the truth."[4] Therefore, truth is the plumbline for the prophetic definition for your life. Please do not confuse having a prophetic definition with being a prophet in a ministry. If you have not been anointed and appointed by God to be a prophet, do not declare that you are one.

In the Old Testament, prophets had a practical office to discharge. It was part of their commission to show the people of God "their transgressions and the house of Jacob their sins" (Isaiah 58:1; Ezekiel 22:2; 43:10; Micah 3:8). They were, therefore, pastors and ministerial monitors of the people of God. It was their duty to admonish and reprove, to denounce prevailing sins, to threaten the people with the terrors of divine judgment, and to call them to repentance. They also brought the message of consolation and pardon (see Isaiah 40:1-2). They were the watchmen set upon the walls of Zion to blow the trumpet, giving timely warning of approaching danger (see Ezekiel 3:17; 33:7-9; Jeremiah 6:17; Isaiah 62:6).

In New Testament times the prophetic office was continued. Our Lord is frequently spoken of as a prophet (see Luke 13:33; 24:19). He was and is the great Prophet of the Church. There was also in the Church a distinct order of prophets (see 1 Corinthians 12:28; Ephesians 2:20; 3:5), who made imparted revelations from God. They differed from the teacher, whose office it was to impart truths already revealed.

Being a prophet is an office ordained by God, and should be confirmed by the leaders in your fellowship of believers. However, every kingdom man has prophetic definition as it relates to speaking truth in a situation and prophesying hope. He speaks the truth to his wife, children, relatives, neighbors, coworkers, and friends. In his workplace he upholds a standard of integrity according to God's Word, and this can be accomplished with politeness and professionalism. In his community he takes an authoritative stand for truth when decadence and confusion try to invade and rule. Telling the truth might make your family, politicians, community leaders, neighbors, and co-workers angry and upset, but always speak the truth.

The Kingdom Man Defined as a Propitiator

The baptism of Jesus Christ possessed tremendous implications and spiritual significance. When the Father pronounced that Jesus was His Son and that He was well-pleased with Him, Jesus received full definition. Not only was He a priest and prophet, but He also bore the definition of a propitiator. In general, a propitiator is one who stands in the gap on behalf of someone else. A propitiator serves as a diplomat who represents, acts, and speaks on behalf of another for the purpose of establishing right relationship and restored order.

Jesus' act of propitiation to God cannot be reproduced by any human being in any time or situation because He is the sole propitiation to God for sin. His sacrifice on the cross once and for all time made propitiation to God and God was completely satisfied that the eternal debt for sin was paid in full. 1 John 2:2 says, "And he is the propitiation for our sins: and not for ours only, but also for the sins of the whole world."

Believers can do nothing to add or subtract from this work of propitiation by Jesus Christ. We can intercede to God on behalf of others, we can forgive others, we can mediate the differences between believers, but we cannot appease God for the sins of others. Only Jesus satisfies God's judgment against sin and makes it possible for all human beings to be saved.

The kingdom man is a propitiator because he is literally placed between time and eternity, understanding how to serve and be a part of the two. Like Jesus, the propitiator's work involves understanding the divine mysteries and the decreed benefits of heaven, while also understanding everyday life and the decreed benefits of earth. Most importantly, he does this with the same standard in which Jesus was our propitiator: unconditional love. First John 4:10 tells us, "Herein is love, not that we loved God, but that he loved us, and sent his Son to be the propitiation for our sins." In whatever situation the kingdom man finds himself, he must do all things by love.

A kingdom man who lives out his definition as a propitiator serves by standing in the gap for his family, community, church, civic organization, and others who need his assistance. He sees his role as simply making life better for another, easing the burden for someone else. A kingdom man is really a man who does not mind becoming a "suffering servant." He will take on the pain of sacrifice and will even deny himself to make certain that life is enhanced for someone else. When a kingdom man gets to this place of maturity, he is truly walking in the way of Jesus Christ.

A kingdom man who is defined as a propitiator understands his role as a provider. He sacrifices his time, energy, and pleasure to make certain that his family is cared for and that he leaves an inheritance to his children and grandchildren. He positions himself to be a lender and not a borrower, to relieve the burden of somebody else.

A kingdom man who is defined as a propitiator makes arrangements for the continuous well-being of his wife, children, supervisor, pastor, and other people God brings into his life. He considers the things that might be irritating to others and eradicates them before they surface. He knows how to stand in the gap between personal agendas and bring unsettled matters into accord, leaving any situation with a God agenda and a peaceful intent.

Consider praying this prayer on a daily basis, so that you can always and eternally be in the right place to make a difference in somebody else's life.

Prayer for a Kingdom Man Defined as a Propitiator

Father, create in me a clean heart, and renew within me a right spirit. Teach me Your ways and Your statutes, so that I can fulfill Your will and not mine. It is through the sacrifice of Jesus Christ that You saved me, redeemed me, and sanctified me. Father, it is my desire to desire more of You, to be in the place where You desire me to be. Help me to bring liberation, solace, peace, justice, and righteousness to every situation in which You place me. I am willing and I am ready to be offered as a sacrifice, to make life better for somebody else.

Spiritual definition is critical for any man who is serious about being a passionate servant in the kingdom of God. Furthermore, once he receives definition from God through His Word, His Spirit, and by the confirmation of leadership, that definition and position in the kingdom is not negotiable. A passionate kingdom man need never be ashamed or intimidated from being all God has defined him to be and doing all God has called him to do.

11

THE DISCERNING KINGDOM MAN

Ye hypocrites, ye can discern the face of the sky and of the earth; but how is it that ye do not discern this time?

Luke 12:56

*I*f there is anything God is wanting to develop in a kingdom man, it is discernment. This is not to be confused with the spiritual gift of discerning of spirits found in 1 Corinthians 12:10, but the godly character trait of discernment that Jesus speaks about in Luke 12:56. The discernment Jesus wants His disciples to have is foundational to the entire Christian life. It is knowing the times and seasons and moves of God, the ability to know what is of God and what is of the enemy in any given situation, and the understanding of the ways of God. Discernment is kin to wisdom, and the Bible commands us to get wisdom, that wisdom is the principal thing (see Proverbs 4:7). You can have passion for God's kingdom, but without discernment you will not be very effective.

Webster's New World College Dictionary defines discernment as "keen perception or judgment."[1] Kingdom men need to cultivate and grow in keen perception and judgment to accomplish their kingdom assignments. For example, as a kingdom man, one of your assignments is to allow the gifts of the Spirit to operate freely in your life.

> *For to one is given by the Spirit the word of wisdom; to another the word of knowledge by the same Spirit;*
>
> *To another faith by the same Spirit; to another the gifts of healing by the same Spirit;*
>
> *To another the working of miracles; to another prophecy; to another discerning of spirits; to another divers kinds of tongues; to another the interpretation of tongues:*
>
> *But all these worketh that one and the selfsame Spirit, dividing to every man severally as he will.*
>
> 1 Corinthians 12:8-11

Yes, the spiritual gifts are given as the Holy Spirit wills, but you are to desire the best gifts and never grieve the Holy Spirit by not allowing Him to use you in this supernatural manner. Discernment is the ability to know when the Holy Spirit desires to use you in this manner.

In the book of 1 Corinthians, Paul seeks to establish God's kingdom order for the operation of gifts and callings in the body of Christ. He writes this to Corinth because he had discerned that the believers there were especially free in operating in spiritual gifts but their services were often reduced to chaos. Paul's intention was to show how the gifts were bestowed to the body for the purpose of bringing unity of purpose and imparting holiness, miracles, and revelation. Never were gifts given to the body to confuse or divide the body of Christ. A discerning kingdom man will understand this and abide in this truth.

Discernment Is Foundational

Discernment, or keen perception and judgment, is foundational for the operation of the nine spiritual gifts listed in 1 Corinthians 12. Any man seeking to develop passion for the kingdom and to participate in the work of the kingdom must develop and pray for discernment in all situations, but most particularly when the supernatural power of God is being released. Consider how discernment enhances every gift.

Word of Wisdom

The word of wisdom is given by the Holy Spirit to impart God's wisdom for an individual in a certain situation or overall condition. The word "wisdom" is the Greek word *sophia*, which means having insight on the true nature of God.[2] With the word of wisdom, the Holy Spirit gives implicit instructions concerning when and how to act in a given situation. One wise writer once stated, "To know what to do is skill, to know how to do is knowledge, to know when to do is wisdom." Discernment coupled with the word of wisdom is an incredible combination. Keen perception and judgment working with the word of wisdom provide the course of action and timing of the Lord that a believer needs.

Word of Knowledge

Knowledge is a gift that allows the body of Christ to have the benefit of understanding the deeper mysteries of God. The person operating in this gift makes a great teacher and does not mind grappling with the difficult issues that others dare not address. Discernment is necessary because every person has a knowledge base from which they are able to share; however, a kingdom man must discern what information should be shared and with whom. A professor I had in seminary stated to us in a class on homiletics, "While preaching you don't have time to tell all you know, you just need to tell the people what they need to know." Keen perception and judgment must accompany a word of knowledge so that the one operating in that gift knows the time and place to share the information the Holy Spirit has imparted.

Faith

Every Christian has faith, but when the Holy Spirit imparts the gift of faith, a believer has an unusual amount of it. Discernment enhances this gift because it tells us that we are operating in a completely different realm of faith for a particular situation. This gift is like a tidal wave of faith moving through us to achieve God's desired purpose in a matter. Keen perception and judgment will know immediately when the gift of faith is imparted by the Holy Spirit into our spirit, and we will immediately and powerfully say and do whatever the Spirit directs.

Healing

In 1 Corinthians 12:9, you will notice that it says "gifts" of healing. Obviously, this means that there is more than one gift of healing. This is because people have a variety of problems that need healing. Some people need physical healing, and within that category of healing are many physical problems. Some people are suffering demonic oppression or possession and need a healing that includes deliverance. Others have mental and emotional wounds that have held them captive and kept them from living in the righteousness, peace, and joy of the Lord. Discernment, or keen perception and judgment, works with this gift to know what particular healing is required and how the Holy Spirit is wanting to bring that healing about.

Miracles

The gift of miracles simply means the ability to function in the supernatural, invoking the power of God to move beyond human reason or natural functions. Jesus performed many miracles that defied nature—all for the glory of God. Therefore, when the Holy Spirit imparts the gift of miracles to us, discernment tells us that this miracle is for one purpose only: to glorify God (not us) in that situation, establishing God's kingdom (not our ministry). I am reminded of the woman with an issue of blood. There was a mob of people pressing in on Jesus, but in Mark 5:30 He discerned that the Holy Spirit was moving: "And Jesus, immediately knowing in himself that virtue had gone out of him, turned him about in the press, and said, Who touched my clothes?" The keen perception and judgment Jesus walked in immediately revealed that a miracle was happening. Like Jesus, we can have the discernment to know when the Holy Spirit is imparting the gift of miracles.

Prophecy

First Corinthians 14:3 says, "But he that prophesieth speaketh unto men to edification, and exhortation, and comfort." To prophesy is to speak the divine revelations of God to an individual, a group, or into a specific situation. A prophecy can pronounce, confirm, and birth us into another season of our lives. A prophecy can give enouragement, direction, correction, and ultimately bring peace and understanding to those who are struggling. All prophecy should be God's truth, what He is saying at that time and place. Discernment attunes us to the mind and will of God so that we know when the Holy Spirit is prompting us to prophesy. We need keen perception and judgment to operate as He wills.

Discerning of Spirits

The spiritual gift of discerning of spirits is when the Holy Spirit reveals what spirit and motive is present in an environment, in a group, or in an individual. This gift enables the kingdom man to know what activity the enemy is establishing, so that he can get the strategy from God to combat and defeat the plan of the enemy. Unlike the character trait of discernment, which is developed over time and study of God's Word and can be present in a believer in all situations, discerning of spirits is given by the Holy Spirit as He wills. Discernment coupled with the spiritual gift of discerning of spirits is a one-two punch to the enemy in any situation!

Tongues

We have already discussed tongues in great detail in Part One. However, the gift of tongues is unique because it is not something the kingdom man activates as he wills (as with his prayer language). The gift of tongues is given as the Holy Spirit wills, and there is an entirely different authority that accompanies this gift. Tongues are a sign for the unbeliever to know that God moves beyond all reason, that He can reach us in ways that we cannot humanly understand or explain. That is why He calls them unknown tongues. How does this happen?

> *Wherefore let him that speaketh in an unknown tongue pray that he may interpret.*
>
> 1 Corinthians 14:13

> *If any man speak in an unknown tongue, let it be by two, or at the most by three, and that by course; and let one interpret.*
>
> 1 Corinthians 14:27

Discernment reveals to us that the Holy Spirit is truly operating the gift of tongues through us or another believer. Keen perception and judgment is able to identify that special authority in the tongue, which is the hallmark of the gift, and then wait for the interpretation to come forth or discern that the Holy Spirit is giving the interpretation to us to give.

Interpretation of Tongues

Interpretation comes from the Greek word *hermeneia*, which is derived from the Greek god Hermes (the Roman counterpart was Mercury). Hermes was a messenger and interpreter of the messages of other gods.[3] This is where we get the word "hermeneutics...The art of finding the meaning of an author's words and phrases, and of explaining it to others."[4] Biblical hermeneutics is to elaborate, to explain, to elucidate, to enlighten, and to expound upon the Scriptures. The one to whom the Holy Spirit imparts the interpretation of tongues is spiritually linked or might be the same believer to whom He gives the gift of tongues. The interpreter brings illumination and explanation. The discerning believer will recognize if he is to give the interpretation and allow the Holy Spirit to use him, or if he is to merely wait for someone else to give the interpretation.

The discerning believer will have a sense of God's timing and purpose in all the operation of the gifts of the Spirit. He is continually walking in keen perception and judgment to know when and how the Holy Spirit desires to operate any of the gifts of the Spirit through him or others. And he is always seeking the best gifts because he has a passion for his kingdom purpose.

Scenarios Illustrating Discernment

David: Discernment of Danger

David was anointed king by the prophet Samuel and appointed by God to replace King Saul. In 1 Samuel 18 the Bible tells us that Saul became extremely jealous of David, who had gained great popularity after defeating the Philistine giant Goliath. When David defeated Goliath, the women got together and made up a song that said, "Saul hath slain his thousands, and David his ten thousands" (1 Sam. 18:8). Verses 8-9 indicate that Saul was extremely angry and kept a jealous eye on David from that day forward.

And Saul saw and knew that the Lord was with David, and that Michal Saul's daughter loved him.

And Saul was yet the more afraid of David; and Saul became David's enemy continually.

1 Samuel 18:28,29

Saul not only kept an eye on David, but he began to try to take his life. One night when David was playing his harp, Saul threw a javelin at David. (See 1 Sam. 18:10-11.) David escaped but became aware that Saul was becoming a dangerous enemy. Next, Saul sent servants to David's house to kill him while he was asleep in his bed. Michal, David's wife and Saul's daughter, warned David and helped him escape through a window, telling him to run for his life. Then Michal took an image, coated it with goat hair, and covered it with sheets in David's bed. When the servants showed up to kill David, they discovered the fake image and realized that David was gone. (See 1 Sam. 19:11-16.)

Days later Jonathan, the son of Saul, invited David to the Feast of the New Moon. This was a time to dedicate the next month to God, and the feast was often celebrated with a meal. David discerned that it was at this feast that Saul would seek to kill him, and he declared to Jonathan:

Thy father certainly knoweth that I have found grace in thine eyes; and he saith, Let not Jonathan know this, lest he be grieved: but truly as the Lord liveth, and as thy soul liveth, there is but a step between me and death.

1 Samuel 20:3

David did not attend the feast, and his life was spared because he had discerned danger. Every kingdom man must develop discernment in order to know when danger is present. There are many men who are in trouble or even incarcerated today because they did not have that keen perception or judgment to detect or sense a dangerous situation. The enemy is shrewd enough to set traps and entice men into a place or position that looks safe and secure, and when they finally realize that they have fallen into a trap it is too late.

Staying safe through discernment is another key reason to maintain your kingdom passion. When you are passionate for the kingdom, you will be continually in prayer, and God can reveal any dangerous scenarios the enemy is trying to orchestrate in your life. Then, like David, you will sense the times of danger and be able to flee.

Discernment will keep you from falling into traps of the enemy that lead to an adulterous affair or a sexually promiscuous lifestyle. It will keep you away from people and places where there is the illegal sale of drugs or alcohol or gambling. Discernment can even keep your life free of crimes such as tax evasion or falsifying documents. The enemy is tricky and seeks to destroy you. Therefore, you must discern his every move in your life and make godly decisions. Let the enemy know that he has no authority over you or those who concern you.

Growing up as a boy I loved to watch the cowboy western television show *The Wild, Wild West*. The hero, James West, would often find himself in a gunfight, or what they called a "showdown." The showdown began with his back against his enemy's back, and then they would proceed to walk a few steps away from each other. After walking a few paces the two would turn to face one another at the same time, draw their weapons, and fire. In all the episodes, James West never lost a showdown simply because he was a master at drawing his gun and firing first. God has given us a mighty weapon called discernment so that we can know times of danger and draw first, taking our enemy down before he can harm us or our loved ones.

Paul and Silas: Discernment of Evil

> And it came to pass, as we went to prayer, a certain damsel possessed with a spirit of divination met us, which brought her masters much gain by soothsaying:
>
> The same followed Paul and us, and cried, saying, These men are the servants of the most high God, which show unto us the way of salvation.
>
> And this did she many days. But Paul, being grieved, turned and said to the spirit, I command thee in the name of Jesus Christ to come out of her. And he came out the same hour.
>
> Acts 16:16-18

En route to fulfill their kingdom assignment, Paul and Silas were confronted by a little girl possessed by a spirit of divination. Divination or fortune telling was very popular in the Graeco-Roman culture, and it generated an extraordinary amount of money. Grieved that the demon controlling the girl was trying to exalt them as God's servants, Paul did not just deliver this girl from a spirit of divination. By casting the demon out of her, he also separated himself from any occult practices. If he and Silas had received the flattery of the girl and allowed the demon to continue, they would have entered into fellowship with it themeslves.

The lesson that every kingdom man must learn from this account of Paul and Silas is that a kingdom man must discern evil activity in people and places not only to get a person delivered but to keep themselves pure and holy and set apart for God. Demonic spirits have a way of surfacing in various and sundry ways, and it is the kingdom man's responsibility to discern them as they try to attack and invade their families, ministries, relationships, communities, and workplaces.

I am not suggesting that you become obsessed with the demonic like a "ghostbuster" and draw negative attention. What I am suggesting is that once you discern a demonic influence is at hand, rebuke it and take authority over it in the name of Jesus and get rid of it. The name and blood of Jesus gives you all power and authority over the devil and his demons, so when you discern the enemy's presence, don't hesitate to evict him from the territory God has given to you.

> The earth is the Lord's, and the fulness thereof; the world, and they that dwell therein.
>
> Psalm 24:1

It is important that we keep our discernment sharp because we live in a culture where the demonic is made to appear friendly and not evil. For example, the *Harry Potter* book and movie series has become a favorite among children and adults.

Harry Potter teaches our children to call on other powers than God for help. Witchcraft, mind control, and demonic manipulation are presented in an entertaining format, which is why the Church should be very concerned. The enemy often uses entertainment to provide a gateway for demonic strongholds to be built into our minds. Kingdom men should discern this evil strategy and not only pray against it but bring biblical awareness of its danger to their families, friends, schools, bookstores, movie theatres, and wherever it seeks to raise its ugly head.

Jesus: Discernment of Transformation

We began this chapter with Jesus saying to the Jewish leaders, "How is it that ye do not discern this time?" (Luke 12:56). Discernment of the times and seasons of God is one of the kingdom man's most valuable weapons, especially when God is bringing us through a difficult trial and testing to get us to the next level of spiritual maturity and transform us into the image of Jesus Christ.

One of the most difficult issues to deal with but something that we all must go through to be transformed is that of betrayal. Even Jesus had to experience betrayal by those He loved, prayed for, and cared for. In Luke 22 we find Jesus seated at the table eating the Last Supper with the disciples. He stops the flow of conversation by declaring, "But, behold, the hand of him that betrayeth me is with me on the table" (Luke 22:21).

Jesus did not discern that somebody was about to betray Him because I believe He knew what Judas was going to do. What Jesus discerned was the timing of God. It was time for

Him to be betrayed. It was time for Him to be crucified. It was time for Him to die and be resurrected. The transformation from Suffering Servant to King of the Universe was beginning and Jesus discerned it.

Jesus knew that the betrayal of Judas would usher Him into His season of transformation. Jesus never became angry with Judas, but He prayed for him to be forgiven and restored. And that is what we must do when we are betrayed. You say, "But how can I do this? This is painful. This is hard." When we discern our time of transformation, the betrayal loses its sting and power over us. As we submit to what God is doing in our lives, we can then forgive those who betrayed us. Jesus is our example in this.

It is important that every kingdom man discerns when God is sending him through a transformation process. When you discern God's process of transformation, you will begin to understand why you are suffering betrayal or other kinds of uncomfortable and painful experiences. You will begin to understand why some friends are not in your life now, why you changed jobs, why you are in living in a place that is not big enough to house your music equipment or your weightlifting set.

You are being transformed, and as soon as you discern this, you will begin to accept the process and not fight against it, deny it, or shun it. Learn to discern the spiritual place of growth in which God has placed you and know that you are there for a purpose. He is transforming you into the image of His Son, and when you have endured and come through it, you will feel like you have been resurrected to a new life.

12

THE DECISIVE KINGDOM MAN

I began Part Two, "The Kingdom Passion of a Man," with the statement, "Manhood and destiny are determined by decisions." We saw how the decisions a man makes impact his life. Now we want to take this full circle and see that the decisions he makes affect everyone around him as well.

Do you realize that many people are depending on you for a decision? Some are looking for hope, while others need a second chance, direction, or perspective. And they are depending on your decision to bring these things to fruition. Whether you are providing leadership in your home, church, workplace, or community, your decisions are vital and important. To be a kingdom man with passion is to understand that every decision you make affects your life and the lives of others. Therefore, it behooves you to make sound decisions, decisions that consider the future while having a positive impact on the present. This is wisdom.

If any of you lack wisdom, let him ask of God, that giveth to all men liberally, and upbraideth not; and it shall be given him.

But let him ask in faith, nothing wavering. For he that wavereth is like a wave of the sea driven with the wind and tossed.

For let not that man think that he shall receive any thing of the Lord.

A double minded man is unstable in all his ways.

James 1:5-8

Kingdom men who make wise, firm decisions first seek the counsel of the Word and the Spirit of God. Only that knowing deep in our spirits that clearly reveals what God's will is for a person or situation will enable us to make a decision in which we are totally secure and confident. When we make decisions hastily, with no thought, no prayer, and no counsel from wise elders, our decisions can be filled with insecurity and doubt. This leads to double-mindedness, which causes us to be unstable and oftentimes destroys any faith we have for the success of the decision we just made. Furthermore, it diminishes the confidence others have in us with regard to that decision.

We all want to do what God desires for us to do, but there are times when we make decisions contrary to His will. Sometimes we do this out of innocence and ignorance; sometimes we do this because we act too quickly and don't ask God for His direction; and then sometimes we get an attitude and just do what we feel like doing, which usually brings disaster. However, God is always there to pick up the pieces of our lives, put us back together, and get us back on track. Kingdom men who have a passion to serve God with pure hearts will ultimately get where God wants them to go because He will see to it.

I find that what impedes a good decision is any instability after the decision is made. That is why it is so important to know that you know that you know that you have heard God's will on the matter. It is the wavering back and forth that drives your wife up the wall. It is your instability that makes your children quietly question if their father really knows what he is doing. When you stand as a leader in your church, workplace, or community and appear uncertain about your decisions, don't expect too much faith from your followers.

Why is indecisiveness a problem for so many men? They are not sure what God's will is and they are even more uncertain about what their own will is. Decisions must be based on knowing what God wants and thus what you want—which sometimes means conforming your will to His. Once you know for certain what God wants and you come into full agreement with Him, making the decision and standing firm on it will be clear.

No story illustrates the power of a decision like the one Jesus told of the prodigal son. This account in Luke 15 is said to be the most tender story ever recorded in history. A man has two sons, and the younger of the two asks his father for his inheritance now instead of after his father dies. The father gives his son his inheritance, and the son leaves his father and his home to find fame and fortune in the world.

And not many days after the younger son gathered all together, and took his journey into a far country, and there wasted his substance with riotous living.

And when he had spent all, there arose a mighty famine in that land; and he began to be in want.

Luke 15:13,14

Instead of using his inheritance wisely, however, the son spends his money on "riotous living." The Greek word for "riotous" is *asotia*, which means, "Having no hope of safety; extravagant squandering, dissoluteness, prodigality...a prodigal is one who spends too much, who slides easily under the influence of flatterers and the temptations with which he has surrounded himself into spending freely on his own lusts and appetites."[1] This story has been traditionally titled "The Prodigal Son" because the word "prodigal" means to spend lavishly and selfishly. Therefore, a backslider returning to the Lord may not be a prodigal if he hasn't spent all his money lavishly and selfishly. We often misuse this term in the Church because we mistakenly associate "prodigal" with leaving the fold and living in sin instead of wasting the resources God gave them.

And he went and joined himself to a citizen of that country; and he sent him into his fields to feed swine.

And he would fain have filled his belly with the husks that the swine did eat: and no man gave unto him.

And when he came to himself, he said, How many hired servants of my father's have bread enough and to spare, and I perish with hunger!

*I will arise and go to my father, and will say unto him, Father,
I have sinned against heaven, and before thee,*

*And am no more worthy to be called thy son: make me as one
of thy hired servants.*

Luke 15:15-19

When the prodigal son spent his entire inheritance, he found himself in the most deplorable condition for a Jew. They were to have nothing to do with swine because God's Law declared that they were unclean animals. The prodigal son was feeding swine. In a real sense, this boy came face to face with his sinful state. And then something amazing occurred. He "came to himself" and said, "I will arise and go to my father." It is after he realized the condition that he was in that this young boy made a radical decision. This boy was not afraid to be decisive. When he made a decision, he went all the way with it.

Some time ago I preached a sermon on this story entitled, "The Good Side of a Bad Boy." Whether his decisions were good or bad, the prodigal son made them firmly and decisively. And eventually, because his heart was purified through his tests and trials, he turned back to God and made a good life for himself. His journey constituted a series of decisions that every kingdom man has to make, and we can all learn from them.

The Decision To Risk

We often shame the young boy for losing his inheritance, but an admirable quality in this young man was that when he was broke, at least he decided to go get a job. He wasn't too proud to feed swine in order to survive and take responsibility for his circumstances. He risked the ridicule and condemnation of his own people to do the right thing.

There comes a time as a kingdom man that you must make a decision to take a "productive risk." I use the word *productive* because not all risks are productive. Some are simply destructive. Taking a destructive risk involves folly; taking a *productive* risk involves faith. In this scenario of taking a productive risk, the plan and will of God is not real clear at a time when you must move forward. There are times when living for God is much like driving through a night of London fog. You don't know that a stop sign is there until you get right up to it.

Paul says that we see though a glass darkly, and we know in part. (See 1 Cor. 13:12.) But there are times we must continue to go forward regardless of the obscurity and take the risk of veering off the path slightly. We take these risks in light of the wisdom and knowledge and counsel that we have, trusting God to keep us on the path, which is why they are productive risks and not destructive risks.

Taking a risk simply means that you realize that God has your back. It is when you take the risk to relocate for a better job, operate in the gift God gave you, prepare your financial portfolio for early retirement, discipline your children in a godly way and establish order in your home that I believe God will honor your servant's heart and bring forth your expected outcome. Kingdom men must make decisions to risk.

The Decision To Rise

One of the most remarkable decisions the prodigal son made was when he found himself in the lowest position a Jewish boy could be in—feeding swine. With great wisdom and courage he said, "I will arise and go to my father." I like this young boy because he exemplified the true meaning of resurrection restitution. He said, "I will arise." This boy came to himself with the revelation that redemption was his only option. He came to himself and knew he could be resurrected through the grace and mercy of his father.

The decision to rise always occurs at a critical time in our lives. There are many men who have made mistakes in the past, and too often they allow the past to haunt them and keep them bound and oppressed. Perhaps you made a quick decision without thinking it through, and that decision cost you your job, your family, your financial stability, or even your health. Maybe your quick decision caused the death of someone else, or maybe you have to live with another horrifying reality that someone contracted the disease that you have or someone's home was wrecked because of your sinful actions. As a result, you are in your own hog pen of life.

If that is you, let the words and actions of this young boy minister to you. Be reminded that regardless of how low you may be in life, you can make the decision to rise! But I must also warn you that only you can make that decision. Others can make suggestions and give you opportunities, but only you can get yourself up and go to the Father. There comes a time in your life when you get so low that the only way you can go is up! I like the way one prolific writer put it, when he said, "If you fall, fall on your back, because if you can look up, you can get up."

All kingdom men must make the decision to rise at one time or another in their lives, so don't let shame and condemnation win. Be inspired by the prodigal son and make the decision to rise.

The Decision To Return

Of all the decisions the prodigal son made, the very wisest was the one to return to his father. He knew that the only way his life could be set straight was to go to his father and have faith in his father's mercy and grace. This boy chose to take a risk, he chose to rise, then he chose to return home. Home for him was the place of his beginning, his security, his place of unconditional love from his father. And his return home is symbolic for so many men today because home is not an address. It is not a physical location. Home is a place of new beginnings, a place of resurrection, a place of rest and peace and prosperity for the soul—not just the bank account.

Home is being back in the will of God. It is the place of restoration and revival where kingdom passion is rekindled. Home is something that you decide you want. Home has to be the deepest desire in your spirit in order for it to become a reality in your life. But only you can decide to return home.

When I tell a man that it is time to return home, I am saying to that man that it is time for him to get back to the perfect plan God has for his life. It is important for us to go to our brothers who have lost their way and invite them to return home. But sir, whether a brother has come alongside to beckon you to come home or whether you are in a place of isolation and loneliness, you must make the decision to come home to Father God and allow Him to change you. This decision can be made by any man who has not lived up to his covenant rights, who has not complied with God's laws and statutes, and who desires to get back into right relationship with God and others.

It is never too late to pray, "God, I have made some errors. I have strayed. I have faltered. But now it's time for me to come home. It's time for me to get in church, get the Word in my heart, join a ministry, and make life better for somebody other than myself."

I am reminded of a story about a young boy who accidentally was separated from his grandmother. She had adopted him after the death of his parents. After walking the streets for many hours, the town police drove up and asked him if he was lost. The young man responded, "Yes, I'm trying to find my way back home." He was too young to know the street names, and he was too nervous to even remember his grandmother's last name.

The police decided to put the boy in the back seat of the squad car and drive him around town until he saw something familiar. After awhile, the young boy suddenly rose up over the front seat and said to the officers, "If you all can get me to the church with the tall cross on the top, I can find my way home." Next to the church with the cross on the top was the boy's home. Isn't it interesting that even when the boy didn't remember his address or his grandmother's last name, he remembered the church with the tall cross on top?

The cross is the way home, Sir! What Jesus did for you on the cross made a path for you to return to the Father and be restored. If you've never gone home to the Father, now is your time. Repent of your sin, thank Jesus for paying the price for your sin on the cross, acknowledge His resurrection that gives you a new life, and declare that from this day forward Jesus Christ alone is your Lord and Savior. If you've strayed from God and His people, simply return! All kingdom men go through times when their hearts become cold to God and the things of God, and the ones who desire to stay passionate for God's kingdom will decide to return.

Words of Wisdom To Inspire a Godly Decision[2]

Somewhere along the line of our development we discover what we really are, and then we make our decision for which we are responsible. Make that decision primarily for yourself because you can never really live anyone else's life.

Eleanor Roosevelt

He who insists on seeing with perfect clearness before he decides never decides.

Henri Frederic Amiel

If I had to sum up what constitutes a good manager in one word, I would say that everything depends on decisions. And good decisions can turn into a bad one if it is applied too late.

Lee Iacocca

We make our decisions, and then our decisions turn around and make us.

F. W. Boreham

Part Three

~

THE KINGDOM
PASSION OF
A WOMAN

13

THE SALVATION OF A KINGDOM WOMAN

*O*ften when we look at what it means to have passion for the kingdom of God, we neglect the vital role women play in effective ministry. In my years as a pastor, I have seen great women of God do mighty exploits for the kingdom and have incredible passion in carrying out their kingdom assignments. However, I have also seen many women fight the same strongholds year after year and never get a breakthrough. Seeking God for answers, I found the most surprising and simple remedy. Women need a deep understanding and ongoing remembrance of their salvation in Jesus Christ.

The Feminist Movement has been all about freedom and liberation and fulfilling potential right alongside the men. But many women in the world are burned out and disillusioned with what they have fought so hard to obtain. Instead of being exhilarated and fulfilled, they are exhausted most of the time and have no inner peace. God's first answer to women of today is salvation in His Son, Jesus Christ, because salvation is *eternally* about inner peace and freedom and liberation and fulfilling potential. Kingdom womanhood begins with understanding the need for salvation. Then, after being born again, the kingdom woman must explore the full operation of salvation in her life.

> *For I am not ashamed of the gospel of Christ: for it is the power of God unto salvation to every one that believeth.*
>
> Romans 1:16

Salvation is the power of God to the kingdom woman who believes. The word "salvation" is translated from the Greek word *soteria,* which means preservation from danger and apprehension.[1] However, I find few women who live with a mindset and comfort that they are preserved from danger and apprehension. Most women of God experience an ongoing struggle to live in the emotional freedom Jesus purchased for them, and too many deal with bitterness, frustration, anger, depression, low self-esteem, disappointment, fear, and anxiety on a daily basis. Again, I believe the remedy is found in an ongoing revelation of who she is because of her redemption through and in Jesus Christ.

Jesus died on the cross to pay the penalty for our sin, to bear all the wrath of God against mankind's sinful state, and to satisfy God's justice. Sin was paid in full through the blood of Jesus Christ and His sacrifice on the cross. In the salvific process of dying at Calvary, He saved us from sin, snatched us from the pit of hell, made us the righteousness of God in Christ Jesus, and sat us at the right hand of the Father to be joint heirs with Him.

> *But God, who is rich in mercy, for his great love wherewith he loved us,*

Even when we were dead in sins, hath quickened us together with Christ, (by grace ye are saved;)

And hath raised us up together, and made us sit together in heavenly places in Christ Jesus:

That in the ages to come he might show the exceeding riches of his grace in his kindness toward us through Christ Jesus.

Ephesians 2:4-7

Verse 7 states God's ultimate intent in salvation. Forever He will be revealing to us the "exceeding riches of his grace in his kindness toward us through Christ Jesus." In other words, from the time a woman is saved, she begins the awesome journey of discovering who she is in Christ Jesus and enjoying the blessing of His exceeding riches as they are poured into her life. This is not a picture of apprehension and insecurity!

Giving It All to Jesus

In the Old Testament salvation is closely aligned with deliverance. One of the Hebrew words translated "deliver" is *natan,* and it has a very interesting definition. *Natan* means to ascribe, place, lay, or give to someone or something.[2] Whereas in the New Testament salvation is something that comes to us by way of Jesus Christ, in the Old Testament salvation is often depicted as something that comes from us. A picture of this is when Hannah was in the throes of labor, giving birth to the prophet Samuel. After hours of pain and perspiration, with the child at the brink of life and the woman at the brink of death, she delivered a long expected hope of Israel. Later she delivered Samuel into the hands of God as she promised (see 1 Samuel 1:1-28).

From the *natan* perspective, salvation is giving something precious to us into the hands of God. He is willing and ready to take our gift, our sacrifice in some cases, and use it to develop and enhance His kingdom. First John 4:19 says, "We love him, because he first loved us." This verse of Scripture describes how a woman's New Testament salvation brings forth her Old Testament salvation. She is saved from danger and apprehension through the blood of Jesus Christ, which enables her to deliver into the hands of God all that she is, says, does, and has. Her salvation is not only in receiving but in giving.

Romans 12:1 says to "present your bodies a living sacrifice, holy, acceptable unto God, which is your reasonable service." A kingdom woman with a passion for God's purpose for her life must consider what she is willing to give up or ascribe to Jesus every day. Then she can consistently walk in her salvation, in her deliverance, and ultimately fulfill the assignment that God has for her.

What are you willing to deliver to God in order to walk in true liberation?

What baggage are you willing to release to God to be of use in His kingdom?

Many Christian women are haunted by their past but either won't or don't give it up to Jesus. Consequently, they continue to live with guilt, shame, anger, bitterness, and doubt because they did something or were involved in something that was obviously not God's will or plan. They have had abortions, have been sexually promiscuous, were abused by a friend or family member, were divorced, had a drug addiction, or put their children in foster care. These past experiences haunt them day and night, continually reminding them of their sins.

Maybe you are a woman with low self-esteem, which causes you to continue in a cycle of bad relationships and collaborations. Perhaps all your life you have believed a lie told to you by the enemy when you were a child: you are too fat or too skinny, too aggressive or too weak, too dark-skinned or too light-skinned, too mean or too nice—and on and on until you don't like anything about yourself. So you have grown up hiding your true self—or never finding out who you really are—because you just want to fit in with those you care about. You have never known or have lost sight of who you were created to be and what you were created to do.

God is calling for you to have a *natan* experience! Make up your mind that it's time to give some stuff up. It's time to let go of other people's standard and live according to God's standard. It's time for you to wake up and say good morning to the beauty inside of you, to realize that you don't have to suffer continuously because of your past. The Holy Spirit, who sheds the love of God in your heart, is strolling you into a new season. This is a season to discover and develop and deliver into God's hands your gifts, your personality, your ministry, and every aspect of your life so that He can celebrate you and see to it that others celebrate you with Him.

The *natan* experience is described in 1 Peter 5:6: "Humble yourselves therefore under the mighty hand of God, that he may exalt you in due time." Giving it all to Jesus is the same as humbling yourself under the mighty hand of God. And the Holy Spirit is telling you that when you do this, He will exalt you when the time is right—when you can handle it! He will raise up people to bless you, to honor you, and to give back to you more than everything you have given. He will even cause your enemies to be at peace with you. Most important, you will be at peace with Him and with yourself.

Sister, let go and let God! Give it all to Jesus today and experience the joy of your salvation.

14

THE SECURITY OF A KINGDOM WOMAN

One of the greatest character traits of a passionate kingdom woman is security. In a day when world terrorism is a threat to lives everywhere and many people are living in fear, the presence of a woman who walks untroubled is like a light breaking in a dark and foreboding place. But how does a kingdom woman walk in such security?

> *He that dwelleth in the secret place of the most High shall abide under the shadow of the Almighty.*
>
> *I will say of the Lord, He is my refuge and my fortress: my God; in him will I trust.*
>
> Psalm 91:1,2

Passionate kingdom women who walk in the security of Christ are passionate about God's Word. They abide in it. They read it, study it, meditate it, model it, and teach it. Passages of Scripture such as Psalm 91 and the 23rd Psalm are just a few of God's words that they hide in their hearts day and night. In doing this, they build a fortress of faith and trust in God around their hearts so that fear cannot penetrate and overtake them.

Terrorism works by the tactic of fear, and in observing the lives of many women today, it is obvious that the enemy has brought terror to them long before September 11, 2001. So many women today live in fear: fear because of their past, fear of what is going to happen now, and fear concerning their future. As we discussed in the last chapter, conquering emotional turmoil is one of the kingdom woman's greatest challenges, and fear is one of the most difficult emotions and demonic strongholds to overcome. If a woman is going to fulfill her kingdom assignment, it is essential that she knows her security in Christ Jesus and overcome fear.

> *If ye then be risen with Christ, seek those things which are above, where Christ sitteth on the right hand of God.*
>
> *Set your affection on things above, not on things on the earth.*
>
> *For ye are dead, and **your life is hid with Christ in God.***
>
> Colossians 3:1-3 [italics mine]

Secure kingdom women walk daily in the knowledge and understanding that they are hidden with Christ in God. They are safely hidden away in God. Their focus is on heavenly things, their affections are set on things above and not things on the earth, they are dead to themselves, and that means they can walk fully in God's kingdom agenda without fear.

Security in God is essential to operate effectively in God's kingdom because she will encounter many people, practices, opinions, cultures, denominations, and evil spirits as she carries out her kingdom assignments. Whether it is at work, the beauty shop, school, church, or the gym, in the kingdom you will always encounter a variety of personalities whose walk may be different from yours and situations that are challenging and even life threatening. Therefore, a kingdom woman must have within her spirit the reality of her security in God, who created her, made her to be who she is, and keeps her hidden under the shadow of His wings.

This is the image that Esther portrayed when she was summoned to stand before the king. Nothing but her security kicked in. She was described as a beautiful woman whose physical features were above all others, and Esther 2:15 states that she obtained "favor in the sight of all them that looked upon her." Although Persian law stated that the king could not marry a Jew, this did not stop Esther from walking in security toward her future. As a result, the king chose her for his wife. But that was not the complete fulfillment of her destiny.

During her tenure as queen, Esther was faced with a formidable situation when Haman, a respected servant of the king, devised a scheme to kill all the Jews. It was at this time that she had to reveal her true lineage to the king, risking her life to save her people. Despite the opportunity for fear, she displayed great faith and confidence. She moved forward with passion in the security of her bloodline, her appearance, and her future.

Esther Had Security in Her Bloodline

Being a Jew, Esther was certain about her family lineage. She knew that her bloodline went back to Abraham, Isaac, and Jacob; and from there it went back to Adam. She loved her people and was not embarrassed to be a Jew. It was her blood connection that caused her to risk her life to save her people.

Esther's bloodline was more than a family tree, however. Her people were God's chosen people, the ones who would bless all the nations of the earth by bringing forth the Messiah. Her confidence and pride was not only in knowing her family history and where her people came from, but in knowing they were the people of God, set apart for His purposes.

It is true that when you understand who you are historically and biologically, a certain security allows you to stand in any situation. There are many people who have great pride in their family bloodline. Knowing your family history and heritage can enhance your self-esteem, especially if you are born into a family with a great legacy. But there is a legacy greater than your biological and historical one, and that is the legacy of your spiritual family.

When you are born again into the family of the Most High God, you have rich blood! The blood of Jesus Christ cleanses you from all unrighteousness and the Holy Spirit transforms your dead spirit into a live spirit, fully restored and connected to God as His child forever. Moreover, Jesus' natural and spiritual bloodline is that of Abraham, through whom the nations of the world would be blessed. (See Gen. 12:3.) We enjoy the richest family lineage in the family of God.

Secure kingdom women know their spiritual family tree! They know who they are in Christ and what God desires them to be and do. With this understanding they not only exude security and confidence but repel the enemy, who is looking for a weak area to invade their lives. He has watched you since conception, seeking to find areas of weakness. That is why it is so important to become secure in who you are. To develop security in your life, I strongly suggest these four things.

1. Every day affirm yourself, your beliefs, your ideas, and your opinions.

2. Learn to master those things that mastered you in the past.

3. Confront new challenges and broaden your territory with new adventures.

4. Know that God has you where you are not by accident but by His design.

Esther Had Security in Her Appearance

When Esther stood before the king, she also had confidence because she had security about her appearance. If nobody else thought Esther looked good, she knew she looked good.

Now it came to pass on the third day, that Esther put on her royal apparel, and stood in the inner court of the king's house, over against the king's house: and the king sat upon his royal throne in the royal house, over against the gate of the house.

And it was so, when the king saw Esther the queen standing in the court, that she obtained favour in his sight: and the king held out to Esther the golden sceptre that was in his hand. So Esther drew near, and touched the top of the sceptre.

Esther 5:1,2

Esther put on her *royal* apparel, and I contend that her outward royalty was a reflection of her inner royalty. Of all the beautiful women in the world, the king chose Esther because she knew she was a child of God, of a spiritual royal line that had no rival in the natural realm. She walked and talked and carried herself like a queen before she ever became an earthly queen. And, although she never compared herself to the other women, she was the most pleasing to the king. She knew God had made her the way she was—body, soul, and spirit—for a reason, and she was fully secure in her appearance.

In life you will always encounter women whom you admire and even envy because you think they are more good-looking, have a more beautiful smile, or have a better-shaped body. But when you get a revelation of being royalty in your spirit, that royalty will begin to manifest on the outside. You'll begin to love yourself for who God created you to be, inside and out, and be secure in how you look.

You may not have teeth that are perfect, but you must smile anyway. You may not be able to afford name-brand clothes, but clean the clothes you have and wear them. You may not be able to get your hair cut and styled every week, but God doesn't require a fresh cut to fulfill His purpose. In whatever fashion you show up, be the best you that you can be and be yourself! Most important, know that God is well pleased with you.

> *Esther was brought also unto the king's house, to the custody of Hegai, keeper of the women...and he speedily gave her her things for purification,...she had been twelve months, according to the manner of the women, (for so were the days of their purifications accomplished, to wit, six months with oil of myrrh, and six months with sweet odours, and with other things for the purifying of the women).*
>
> Esther 2:8,9,12

In this passage of Scripture we see that Esther also did everything she knew to do and was told to do to make herself beautiful for the king. In fact, she spent months purifying herself on the inside and the outside, making herself look as good as possible. Just because God created you to be royalty inside and out doesn't mean there aren't things you can do in the natural to enhance your beauty. Some Christian denominations teach that it is not permissible for kingdom women to wear make-up, jewelry, and fashionable clothes. But if God blesses you with some nice things that are tasteful and modest, I believe it is all right to use them. Esther was a beautiful woman, but she still picked out the best dress she had when she stood before the king.

I encourage you to take a good look at yourself in the mirror of God's Word and let the Holy Spirit be your chamberlain. Let Him tell you where and how you need to make changes and improvements—inside and out. Then follow His instructions as closely as Esther followed Hegai's and see if you don't have more security and confidence about your appearance.

Your appearance preaches sermons to unbelievers before you invite them to church. You are a representative of the King, and your appearance needs to reflect modesty, holiness, discipline, self-respect, and the calling God has on your life. You will not only fulfill your kingdom assignments with greater joy and confidence, but you will do it with the grace and beauty of a queen.

Esther Had Security in Her Future

One of the issues that continues to haunt many of our women today is summed up in the question, "What will my future hold?" This is the question raised by the teenage girl who is leaving middle school for high school, the college graduate looking for a job in the workforce, the middle-aged mother seeing her children leave home to get married and follow God's path for them, and the retired woman wondering how her life will end.

The future can be frightening because it is unknown. It is the unknown that sends our security sensors into flight and fear. Therefore, when this issue is raised, we must remind ourselves that the same God who was with us in our past, who is with us now in our present, is the same God who will be with us in our future.

> *Be content with such things as ye have: for he hath said, I will never leave thee, nor forsake thee.*
>
> *Jesus Christ the same yesterday, and to day, and for ever.*
>
> Hebrews 13:5,8

The Scripture declares that we are called to walk by faith, that our attitude toward any challenge, including the future, should be of faith and trust in the Lord. He commissions us to live just as hopeful about our future as we are about our present and our past, and one of the truths that enables us to do this is the very consistency and constancy of God. While our future may be unknown to us, it is known to Him. He is omniscient, and He is the same today as He was yesterday, and He will be the same forevermore. He will never leave us or forsake us, now or in the future.

What made Esther a heroine is her attitude toward her future. She laid it all down for God. She was so convinced that she existed for her people and not herself that her future became secondary to the future of her people. Initially she thought that becoming queen was her kingdom assignment, but that was just the beginning. Saving her people was her ultimate kingdom assignment. Her future was the future of her people.

When Haman successfully orchestrated an evil scheme to make it lawful to kill Jews, the king was unaware that his beloved queen, Esther, was also a Jew. Esther was the Jews' only hope, but to save them she would have to tell the king she was a Jew and beg for mercy for her people. This could cost her her life. Her response reveals everything she believed and actually was.

> Go, gather together all the Jews that are present in Shushan, and fast ye for me, and neither eat nor drink three days, night or day: I also and my maidens will fast likewise; and so will I go in unto the king, which is not according to the law: and if I perish, I perish.
>
> Esther 4:16

This kind of passion and courage is what happens when you are consumed with a cause and a purpose bigger than you. Nothing but the assignment matters. This is not to suggest that kingdom women should never give attention to anything but their kingdom assignment in ministry. Even Esther was still disciplined and diligent to keep her spirit edified, her emotions under control, her health strong, and her perspective balanced. But when the time came to lay everything on the line, her own security was so completely in God and the mission He had called her to that she forgot about herself. That is the ultimate security in God—to forget about yourself.

> *Then said Jesus unto his disciples, If any man will come after me, let him deny himself, and take up his cross, and follow me.*
>
> Matthew 16:24

Everybody is willing to grab the cross, but picking it up and following in the sufferings of Christ is another thing. Following in the sufferings of Christ means denying yourself. And just what does denying yourself and following Christ have to do with having security about your future? Jesus is in it! He's leading you and you cannot go anywhere He doesn't go first. Whatever your future holds will not get to you until it first passes through Jesus. What better security can a woman of God have about her future than that?

Would you want something in your future that doesn't go through Jesus first? Would you want a husband and family, a career, a ministry, or anything that has not been endorsed by Him? This means that wherever He leads you, the blessings that follow are passed on to you from Him. If you stay in His shadow, your future will be secure.

This is not to suggest that your future won't include some days of testings, trials, and disappointments. The enemy is not pleased that you are following Jesus into your future and will do his best to stop you. But even when you have those days of difficulty, you should not be deterred or distracted. Your future is much greater than your trial.

> *For our light affliction, which is but for a moment, worketh for us a far more exceeding and eternal weight of glory;*
>
> *While we look not at the things which are seen, but at the things which are not seen: for the things which are seen are temporal; but the things which are not seen are eternal.*
>
> 2 Corinthians 4:17,18

Know that all of the inheritance of the Lord has not been given to you yet. As you continue to walk in your assignment, God is going to pile up your shopping basket with everything you need to get you where you need to go and provide for the future. Stop worrying and harboring doubt in your heart about what is to come. When it is time for you to get married, Jesus will lead you to your husband. When it is time for you to have a baby, Jesus will bring you to the child. When it is time for you to launch your ministry, Jesus will show you the way. In fact, nothing in God's plan for your life can be stopped as long as you follow Him. Your future is in His mind and it will happen in His time. You will fulfill His purpose, and His purpose will be accomplished His way.

Esther was secure with her future because she knew that whether she lived or died, her life would be celebrated through the sparing of her people. As a matter of fact, the Jews to this day celebrate the Feast of Purim in honor of her great courage that caused them to be spared. This brings us to a wonderful truth: By putting your future on the line to secure the future of others, you secure your own future.

What investment are you making into someone's future? What are you doing to help some child reach her full potential and tap into the gifts that God placed within her? What are you doing to secure the future for a neighborhood or a long-awaited project that will change the lives of people for the better? What are you doing to sustain the longevity of a college, a community development corporation, or even your church? Whatever God calls you to do, you can be an Esther—secure in your bloodline, secure in your appearance, and secure in your future.

15

THE SOCIABILITY OF A KINGDOM WOMAN

*I*t always amazes me how many successful ministers I meet who do not like the people God called them to serve. To me, this is an insult to the kingdom, and it is against everything God intended the kingdom to be. Jesus Himself said that the greatest two commandments were to love God with your whole life and then to love your neighbor as yourself. (See Matt. 22:36-40.) As children of God we are all called to serve one another and to reach out to the lost and serve them. People are the business of the kingdom of God, and the Bible says that God is love, so His kingdom should reflect His character at all times and in all situations.

He that loveth not knoweth not God; for God is love.

And we have known and believed the love that God hath to us. God is love; and he that dwelleth in love dwelleth in God, and God in him.

1 John 4:8,16

The kingdom of God is in the business of loving people. We express God's love by leading them to the Lord, discipling them in the Word, and assisting them in any physical way the Lord leads. This truth is the basis of all social activity in the kingdom of God—everything from marriage to parenting and mentoring to friendship to being neighbors to ministry partners to business associates. All these social relationships should reflect and have as their basis the love of God. In short, passionate kingdom women love the people God has called them to serve.

As you minister there are numerous opportunities to meet people from various nations, cultures, communities, denominations, and socio-economic spheres. As a kingdom woman, it is tremendously important for you to wisely walk in God's love as you form various kinds of relationships and social connections. The concept of the body of Christ being a network of social relationships is not new. Jesus used this analogy of the kingdom in His own teaching.

> *Again, the kingdom of heaven is like unto a net, that was cast into the sea, and gathered of every kind:*
>
> *Which, when it was full, they drew to shore, and sat down, and gathered the good into vessels, but cast the bad away.*
>
> Matthew 13:47,48

Picturing the people of God operating as a global net to bring in the lost to the kingdom gives us a clear understanding of how believers do the work of the kingdom. Jesus illustrated this from the beginning of His ministry, even when He called Peter and some of the other twelve apostles to follow Him. He was preaching about the kingdom of God on the shores of Lake Gennesaret and the crowd was pressing against Him, when He saw two boats that were empty; the fishermen were cleaning their nets after fishing all night. So He climbed into one of the fishermen's boats to continue preaching more effectively to the multitude. The boat He just happened to get into was Simon Peter's. (See Luke 4:43-5:3.)

> Now when he had left speaking, he said unto Simon, Launch out into the deep, and let down your nets for a draught.
>
> And Simon answering said unto him, Master, we have toiled all the night, and have taken nothing: nevertheless at thy word I will let down the net.
>
> And when they had this done, they enclosed a great multitude of fishes: and their net brake.
>
> And they beckoned unto their partners, which were in the other ship, that they should come and help them. And they came, and filled both the ships, so that they began to sink.
>
> Luke 5:4-7

When we read this text, we usually focus on the abundance of the catch; but when we look at it in the light of kingdom sociability, we see something very powerful. I believe the real miracle is that the fishermen who had given up hope of catching any fish came together as partners and began to do real "net" working. Jesus was showing them right from the beginning what it means to be sociable in the kingdom of God.

Sociability has to do with who you allow and who you don't allow to enter your life. It has to do with partnering with other believers to maximize your effectiveness, reach your goals, and accomplish the plan God has for your life. As these men fished together, we see several important principles of sociability operating that women with a passion for the kingdom need to know to be successful.

Common Collaboration

And they beckoned unto their partners.

Luke 5:7

You must learn to trust others to assist you in gathering your abundance, to collaborate with them in carrying out your kingdom assignments. The passionate kingdom woman is so secure that she doesn't mind calling on someone for help or partnering with others to help them carry out God's plan for their lives. I like to look at it this way: God is getting ready to bless you so abundantly that you have to make room on your spiritual ship so others can come onboard and help you gather it in.

Therefore, a kingdom woman can't be controlling, dominating, egocentric, or narcissistic. She must be a woman who knows exactly what God wants and how to tap into the deeper dimensions of God to find out how He wants to get what He wants. Then, when she sees the plan, she is not intimidated to ask others to be a part of what God is doing. When God gives her a dream, a vision, and a plan, the next step is to pray and believe for the right people to come in and partner with her in her new business, ministry, or family adventure.

On the other hand, if a kingdom man or woman approaches you and asks you to be a part of their dream, vision, and the plan of God for their life, a passionate kingdom woman is not afraid to link with other people of faith and serve them as long as the Lord leads her. She knows that in serving others and helping them to fulfill their kingdom assignments, she is investing in the fulfillment of her own kingdom assignments.

A passionate kingdom woman is not afraid of admitting to her partners that she doesn't know how to do everything God has called her to do, especially when He begins to load her boat with all kinds of opportunities. She is really going to need some help then! She's got to discern the people God has placed in her life to facilitate His plan and eradicate any fear that everyone is out to get her or they are giving superficial support until they can take her plan and implement it themselves. If God brought them to her, then He will see that they do right by her, or He will take them away and bring someone else.

Common collaboration means that there are divinely appointed spiritual partners for different areas of your life, and when they show up, you must allow them to partner with you and help you. While it is important that you remain open for this kind of kingdom partnership, I must warn you that everybody is not ready for this kind of collaboration. I will say again that you must be wise and discerning in letting people into your life.

Again, the kingdom of heaven is like unto a net, that was cast into the sea, and gathered of every kind:

Which, when it was full, they drew to shore, and sat down, and gathered the good into vessels, but cast the bad away.

Matthew 13:47,48

Notice that once the net was drawn the fishermen would throw away the bad fish. This illustrates to me the principle of choosing your partners with wisdom and discernment. It is what Paul admonished the Galatians about when he warned them concerning the Judaizers. They were a sect of Jewish believers who followed Paul wherever he went to uproot his teachings. Judaizers were instruments of doubt, pessimism, deceit, destruction, malady, and non-productivity—and people like that will show up to crash your party today. That is why it is important to be prayerful and have total peace when you choose those who will partner with you in life and in your ministry or business.

I am always fascinated with the story of Mary and Elizabeth. When Mary was pregnant with Jesus and Elizabeth was pregnant with John, there was a divine unction in both of them to meet and collaborate. These were two pregnancies that changed the entire course of human history, and the significance of the pregnancies was evident prior to the births of John and Jesus.

Pregnancies are always a time of tremendous joy and transition, but these two pregnancies were even more significant. Mary and Elizabeth were first cousins and both had endured several months of protruding stomachs. When Mary arrived to meet Elizabeth and issued her salutation and greeting, their babies leaped in their wombs. This is not only a *kairos*, or prophetic,[1] moment, but it illustrates what makes a collaboration "common." When partnering or collaborating with someone else, it is wise to find someone who is pregnant like you are.

When you collaborate with someone who has a common experience, vision, goal, and godly ambition, it is much easier to be like-minded in the Spirit and maintain unity. Look for partners who are pregnant with possibilities, vision, optimism, determination, fortitude, tenacity, and ability like you are. If someone has never been pregnant and doesn't understand what it is to be pregnant, you are going to have a greater challenge getting them to understand what God has called you to do and how He wants you to do it. I believe commonality really happens when you connect with someone who is pregnant just like you are.

As you contemplate collaboration with those who come alongside you and try to determine which ones God brought and which ones the enemy brought or which ones just don't know what they're doing, here are some questions that can aid you in discernment so that you can choose your partners wisely.

- What does this person have in common with my life?

- What has this person done in the past to merit being a part of our future?

- What are this person's strengths and weaknesses?

- What does this person need to satisfy and fulfill our lives?

- What ideas does this person have about the goal that we are trying to accomplish?

- What indication does this person have that they are also assigned to assist me in my effort?

Partner Productivity

Recently in the State of North Carolina two major banks merged and became one bank. The fundamental idea behind a merger is simply this: "Together we can do more." Corporations merge and become conglomerates in order to dominate a market. Instead of four companies vying for a share of the market, each company struggling to survive, they merge to form one company that corners the market. It is also easier for a larger company with more resources available to make inroads into the markets of competitors and untapped markets. A very shrewd CEO knows that a market can be dominated through mergers and acquisitions.

In the kingdom of God I call this partner productivity. When two or more believers come together in a common cause, the combination of unity and greater numbers multiplies their ability to produce what God has called them to produce. This is a vital principle for passionate kingdom women who are called to make a difference in this world because it is a very cold, brutal world in which to battle and press forward alone.

Statistics show that there has been an increase of women who are doing well in the workforce, rising on the corporate scene, and developing entrepreneurial businesses. They are doctors and lawyers who are opening their own offices. They are forming telemarketing enterprises, operating beauty salons, organizing computer technical assistance groups, and the list goes on. Unfortunately, too many have been hindered by the notion, "If it is going to happen, I have to do it myself."

Many of these women have known great rejection and resistance, sometimes just because they are women. Others are single women whose husbands left them without financial support for themselves or their children. They are widows who are older and have been doing the important work of being wives and mothers but now find themselves alone and without any training for the workplace. Worst still, the Church really doesn't know what to do with these women. Thus, even kingdom women tend to believe, "It's just me and Jesus."

While there are times when you must be able to stand on your own in certain situations, when you get a dream, a vision, or a plan from God you must understand the power of partner productivity. When the disciples were out fishing and they followed the instructions of Jesus, they were so blessed with an abundance of fish that they had to call for their partners. This suggests some fundamental principles to consider with regard to partner productivity.

Realize Your Limitations

The disciples realized their limitations. They knew they could not pull that many fish in the net by themselves. They knew they needed some help. If you are going to be a kingdom woman, you must understand that that there are times when you don't know it all, can't think it all, and certainly can't do it all. If you are a woman who has a vision or an idea that you feel

God has placed within your spirit, but you are afraid to step out because you didn't complete high school, graduate from college, or have the training or the financial resources it takes to get that baby birthed; know that God has never been short on resources or people who can do what you can't do and figure out what you can't figure out.

If you want to start your own community development corporation but don't have the slightest idea of where to begin, God always has an attorney somewhere to advise you on what needs to happen to get this underway. If you have a business you want to launch and God has blessed you with an entrepreneurial spirit, He will send people your way to tell you how to do and where to do it.

Every time you purchase something from a business like the one you want to start or that is related to it, never miss an opportunity to speak to the manager or owners if they are available. Have your questions ready and a notebook handy. You will be surprised at how small the circuit is and how willing they will be to give you the benefit of their experience and knowledge. If you have a ministry that you are trying to birth, there are many believers you can talk to, beginning with your pastor, or there might be a conference that has the same focus that you have.

Partner productivity requires you to know your limitations. If you are not an organizer, surround yourself with those who have this ability. If you are not a financial expert, develop a circle of advisors who can assist you or do it for you. If you are not a writer, find someone who knows how to put your ideas on paper. But by all means, do not allow your limitations to hinder your going forward with the vision and the plan that God has placed within you. Partner productivity means that you know how to say, "Help!"

Selfless Sanctification

Partner productivity is not just sharing the work and the responsibility but also sharing the blessings. Selfless sanctification involves giving to others as God has given to you, not just in terms of wealth but in terms of knowledge, wisdom, experience, education, love, acceptance, and encouragement. Selfless sanctification makes partner productivity a kingdom activity that manifests the character of God by showing His love to others.

Some years ago I ministered in a crusade in Haiti. I will never forget going into an area where we were told not to give the children anything out of our pockets. As we entered this village community, the dirt from the dusty roads saturating the air, I saw huts with only a piece of metal to serve as a roof and cardboard to serve as walls. I had never seen a place so thoroughly littered with rubbish and trash. Pigs, dogs, and goats lived in the huts with the people. I saw a toddler, ribs showing through her skin, take a bath in a puddle of water and get out of that puddle as if she were the cleanest thing alive.

When I saw this devastation, my heart broke and emotionally I was no good. Someone must have told the children we were coming because they came from everywhere with their hands out. Initially I followed the instruction of our guide, and we turned the children away. But then there was one young boy who insisted, and when I looked into his eyes God began to show me that the hope for this boy's future was dependent upon how I responded to him. He showed me in his eyes that so many people had turned him away, and that one more rejection would be the very thing to break the little faith and hope he had for his future. As I gazed into his pleading eyes and saw those white, pearl teeth smiling at me, I reached into my pocket and pulled out a piece of peppermint candy.

The boy took the candy and ran. I thought that at least he could have stayed to show me how much he enjoyed the candy or to thank me! But off he ran. I turned and began to walk away. Then moments later I felt someone tugging on me from behind. When I turned around I saw the same little boy, but now he had a friend with him. He began to point to his candy, and then point to my pocket. It was obvious that he wanted his friend to have the same thing he had. Again I was moved by compassion and gave his friend a piece of candy, expecting them to take off immediately.

To my surprise, this time neither of them ran away, but together they held hands, bowed before me, and said in French, "Merci"—thank you. When they ran this time, I didn't feel a void because I knew if I never saw that boy again in my life, we would always be bonded by a piece of candy, his thank you, and his kindness to share with a friend the blessing that he had received.

That little boy had the same selfless sanctification that the disciples had when they were blessed with the abundant catch of fish. Selfless sanctification says, "God has taken me through a process, and the blessings He's given me are not just for me but for others." God never has a shortage on provision, resources, or wisdom, and kingdom women are to bless others as God has blessed them. This is true in every area of their lives.

> *Older women likewise are to be reverent in their behavior, not malicious gossips, nor enslaved to much wine, teaching what is good, that they may encourage the young women to love their husbands, to love their children, to be sensible, pure, workers at home, kind, being subject to their own husbands, that the word of God may not be dishonored.*
>
> Titus 2:3-5 NASB

What would the kingdom of God look like if passionate kingdom women practiced selfless sanctification? They would be sharing their lives and pouring all they have and know into the younger women who are trying to find their way in God's kingdom as godly wives, mothers, ministers, and professionals in the workplace.

What would the kingdom look like if passionate kingdom women who had been in prison began to mentor juvenile delinquent teenagers about the real world of crime? What would the kingdom look like if passionate kingdom women who were successful in a profession taught a Bible study about women in the marketplace and poured all their experience and stories of falling down and getting up and giving to others into women who were just beginning to venture into a new business or profession? What would the kingdom look like filled with passionate women who knew the value of selfless sanctification, who realized that what they have to offer is a reflection of what they have already gained, and now they're just looking for someone to give it to?

Whether the subject is marital peace and joy, the birthing of a child or ministry or business, or the operation of spiritual gifts, passionate kingdom women don't just experience God by themselves. They partner with other women to give them the benefit of all they have been through and learned. They teach how they did it, how they moved beyond obstacles and challenges, how they persevered and endured hardship, how they beat the odds, and how they overcame discouragement and defeat again and again.

Partner productivity is simply understanding that together we can accomplish more. It is realizing our limitations and not being afraid to ask for help. And it is developing selfless sanctification, which not only shares the financial benefits but all the wisdom, love, and hope of our lives with others.

Treasured Transformation

When Simon Peter saw it, he fell down at Jesus' knees, saying, Depart from me; for I am a sinful man, O Lord.

For he was astonished, and all that were with him, at the draught of the fishes which they had taken:

And so was also James, and John, the sons of Zebedee, which were partners with Simon. And Jesus said unto Simon, Fear not; from henceforth thou shalt catch men.

And when they had brought their ships to land, they forsook all, and followed him.

Luke 5:8-11

The disciples' lives were radically transformed through this experience with Jesus. "They forsook all and followed him." They desired the One who created and controlled the fish more than they desired the fish. The miracle catch brought them to their knees before a holy, all-powerful God. They saw their sin and were afraid. But Jesus comforted them and told them that from that time on they would not be catching fish but human beings. The transformation that they had experienced in Jesus Christ was the treasure they would pass along to others.

God is always calling us to transformation, even after we are born again. Being born again is the most treasured transformation, as we are freed from Satan's grip, become a new creature in Christ, have God's law written in our hearts, and have a consummate desire to please Him and serve Him all of our lives. Transformation continues to be treasured as we begin to grow in the Word, to be more sensitive to the Holy Spirit, and to see ourselves as God sees us.

As a passionate kingdom woman, I encourage you to allow Jesus to use every experience to transform you into someone who looks more like Him than before that experience. Just as He used fish to transform the disciples, He will take something in your life to transform you if you will let Him. When you understand this principle of transformation and allow it to happen to you a few times, you will see why it is such a treasure.

You will begin to see every challenge or blessing as an opportunity for your character and personality to surface so that Jesus can take you from faith to faith and glory to glory. Maybe you are saying to yourself, "How can an abusive relationship, a date rape, an abortion, or a mental breakdown transform me into the image of Jesus?" My answer to you is that God did not cause these misfortunes and traumas. They are the tactics of the enemy. However, God will come into your life to heal you, restore you, and make you whole if you will let Him. Then, as a whole woman, a passionate kingdom woman, you can say, "I can do what God says I can do, be what God says I can be, and go where God says I can go." That's transformation!

Every kingdom woman must understand the purpose of the enemy in her life. He comes to steal, kill, and destroy, but God will take all that the enemy tries to do and use it for your good. The enemy doesn't know it, but his tactics against you will usher you into transformation.

I am always amazed at how early many of us judge our experiences. Too many times we perceive situations as working against us and to our detriment, when actually the challenge the enemy places before us is God's training ground for greatness. He is there to turn that situation for our good and transform us into the image of His Son in the process. This became a reality in my life during the earlier years of pastoring.

In the introduction of this book, I talked about my tumultuous experience in my first pastorate. There was one woman in particular who was vehemently opposed to my leadership. Her actions kept me up many long nights. It wasn't until I began to digest the experience and logic of Joseph that I began to understand why I was going through this trial. Joseph's story is summed up in his statement to his brothers, who had sold him into slavery, "But as for you, ye thought evil against me; but God meant it unto good, to bring to pass, as it is this day, to save much people alive" (Gen. 50:20). While this woman literally tormented our church, in the end I saw that she was the catalyst that transformed my ministry, bringing me to a new realm of maturity and understanding, of prayer and knowledge of God's Word.

God used the tactics of the enemy to establish prayer and fasting as a priority for my life. Kingdom women must meet the obstacles that the enemy sets before them with prayer and fasting in order to keep their passion and focus. Prayer and fasting brings us to the feet of Jesus to get the wisdom and courage and comfort we need to go on. I read somewhere that one of the greatest tragedies of life is not an unanswered prayer but an unoffered prayer. Prayer moves us from solo to symphony with God and therefore neutralizes the effects of a bad situation. Transformation comes as a result of prayer and many times fasting as well.

God used the tactics of the enemy to shape my theology. Theology is merely the study of God, and I began a deeper study of His omnipotence (being all-powerful), omnipresence (existing everywhere at the same time), and omniscience (knowing everything there is to know) when I was under severe pressure. Often it is in the fires of adversity that you gain new insight into the Scripture. Verses that you have read all of your life suddenly have meaning and depth that you never saw before. Sermons I preached before a time of transformation grew into something entirely different after the time of transformation. Again, attacks of the enemy were the catalysts that motivated me to dig deeper into God's Word and grow.

God used the tactics of the enemy to establish a plan for my life and my ministry. The enemy uses tactics that place you in circumstances where the Holy Spirit teaches you to think, contemplate, meditate, and interpret things differently because you are in a different battle that requires a different strategy. And because I went to a new level of understanding of how God wants me to operate, I became more effective. If the enemy had not posed that dilemma and presented that problem, I would not have achieved certain goals, dreams, and desires. You should give thanks to God for the person you know wanted to destroy you because they actually ushered you into a new season of transformation that otherwise you would have never known.

God used the tactics of the enemy to help me really understand the truth about myself. My mother, a woman of great wisdom and humor, teaches me lessons of life at the oddest times and in the oddest moments. In one conversation she said to me, "You can learn anything from anybody." This was not new for me, of course, but then she said, "Even a broken clock is right at least twice a day." This stunned me because she was right, especially when it comes to learning lessons from your enemy. The accuser of the brethren uses the best weapons he can against us, and the best weapons are the truth about our sins, faults, and errors.

If you ever have a discussion with people who are opposing your destiny and are under the influence of the enemy, listen to them. Then take the parts of that discussion that are true and admit them to yourself and to God. Maybe you are a little self-centered. Maybe you do say things the wrong way at times. Maybe you are moving a little too fast. Maybe you didn't use the right procedure or process. Maybe you are the culprit of the downfall in a relationship. Maybe you are little pushy, bossy, conniving, or insulting. Everything the enemy says is not always wrong, and you must face the truth about yourself.

One thing is extremely important when you understand the truth about yourself, however. When you see that something you are doing is not right, the enemy will try to come in and put shame and condemnation on you. Do not let him! Go immediately to God's Word and let the Holy Spirit show you what to pray over yourself in order to repent and be cleansed. God is bringing you to freedom and not to be distressed and devastated because you aren't the perfect person that you thought you were.

God uses the tactics of the enemy to transform you, and when your heart is made stronger and your life is more clearly defined, you will come to the conclusion that the person the enemy worked through was more of a blessing than a curse in your life. A well-known theologian once said, "I don't have enemies. I just have confused friends." When your confused friends help to transform your life, it is a transformation that you will treasure.

Never let go of your testimony of how God transformed you and delivered you. David declared, "Create in me a clean heart, O God; and renew a right spirit within me" (Ps. 51:10). He also said, "Thou preparest a table before me in the presence of mine enemies" (Ps. 23:5). Not only will God prepare a table for you in the presence of your enemies, but He will make the enemy put food on your table!

16

THE SERENITY OF A KINGDOM WOMAN

Where does a kingdom woman find peace and solace for her life? Where does she receive comfort from the painstaking realities of her world? Where is the place her soul is restored, where God soothes the aches and bandages the wounds? Where is it that her spirit can be released to fly as free as a dove? Where is it that she can experience the tranquility of the river of life that flows like silk into a pool of celebration? Where does she go for God to romance her and speak to her about her intentions, emotions, and beliefs? Every kingdom woman needs a place where she can find serenity.

Serenity is what God uses to communicate His presence to us. When we experience His presence, everything falls into place, is set in order, and nothing can disturb us. A woman with kingdom passion must possess this trait because serenity reflects the salvation, security, and sociability she walks in. For this reason, I believe serenity is kin to wisdom, which is simply unlocking the truth behind a false reality. It is when you discover real truth in Christ Jesus and all that He desires to bring into your life that you begin to find serenity and live in it.

In a world where there is much pushing and shoving, spouses demanding certain things, children needing to go to soccer practice, church choir rehearsal, another PTA meeting, getting in shape and staying in shape, and trying to accomplish something that will give you another certificate on your wall, you need to have a place to retreat from the responsibilities of your world and experience God's gift of serenity. Most people think of their church, temple, or synagogue as that place.

Serenity is what Mary and Joseph found in Luke 2:27-39 when they presented baby Jesus to the priests at the Temple in Jerusalem, according to the Law of Moses. When they arrived, they were met by a man by the name of Simeon. He had a covenant with God that he would not see death until he had seen the Messiah. Mary and Joseph went to the Temple to follow the law, but this man went to the Temple by the Holy Spirit to set their hearts at ease that their child, born of Mary's virgin womb, was truly the Son of God.

When Simeon saw Jesus, he took Him in his arms and said, "Lord, now lettest thou thy servant depart in peace, according to thy word: For mine eyes have seen thy salvation" (Luke 2:29,30). He found serenity for his life at this moment, but three things struck me about this confrontation between Simeon and Mary and Joseph. First, Simeon spoke peace and conflict at the same moment. Second, Simeon finds serenity when the promise is connected with the purpose. And third, Simeon and Anna are old in years, but they celebrate serenity by passing it on to the younger generation. These three issues bring great understanding to the kingdom woman who desires to walk in serenity.

Simeon Speaks Serenity and Conflict

And Joseph and his mother marvelled at those things which were spoken of him.

And Simeon blessed them, and said unto Mary his mother, Behold, this child is set for the fall and rising again of many in Israel; and for a sign which shall be spoken against;

(Yea, a sword shall pierce through thy own soul also,) that the thoughts of many hearts may be revealed.

Luke 2:33-35

Serenity can be obtained in the presence of the Lord at all times and through all situations, and this passage of Scripture illustrates this truth. The Holy Spirit not only tells Mary and Joseph that their baby is indeed the Son of God, but prepares them for what is to come. Simeon warns them about the conflicts and the dangers that are ahead for this exceptional Child, who is set for the rise and the fall of many in Israel. Events will occur in the future that will be like a sword piercing Mary's soul.

What we are witnessing in this dramatic moment is Simeon seeking to establish serenity before the time of conflict, not for himself (because he knows he will not live to see it), nor for Joseph (because the Holy Spirit knows he will not live to see it), but for Mary. She is the one who must be strong and maintain serenity through the most heartbreaking thing that can happen to a woman, witnessing the brutal death of her child.

This is a valuable lesson to learn as a kingdom woman. When the Holy Spirit warns you of difficult times to come, you must seek His comfort and serenity. Seek it before the conflict or challenge occurs. Then the enemy cannot attack you from behind, catch you off-guard, and induce you to say and do things that are inappropriate, sinful, or out of God's will. Serenity is not something you only find in the midst of the storm, but it can be what you bring to the storm.

Too many times we wait until a state of emergency or a crisis breaks out in our lives to rush to find serenity in God. And too often, because we are caught off-guard, we try unholy or ungodly ways to help us to find the peace that we need to make it through. Many women in distress will go on shopping sprees, start smoking or drinking again, eat too much, become obsessive about maintaining a clean house, waste time talking on the telephone, turn to promiscuity, or even physically hurt themselves. True serenity cannot come from any of these activities. It can only come from the presence and wisdom of the Lord in their situation. And that serenity can be established before the crisis ever occurs.

Kingdom women maintain their passion by developing serenity every day. They know that they can find serenity daily in prayer, meditation on the things of God, reading and studying God's Word, praising and worshiping the Lord, or having a chat with a believer who is filled with wisdom. Serenity found in the Lord is lasting and strong. It enables women to keep their emotions under control and their lives in godly perspective.

Serenity can be found in a park, in the mountains, at a beach, or in some other relaxing environment—just communing with the Lord. However, it is not the environment that gives you lasting serenity. If that were the case, as soon as you left the environment, you would lose it. You can sit among trees and enjoy serenity for awhile. You can sit on the beach and enjoy the breeze blowing across your face, but lasting serenity won't come from trees or water or wind. You can find temporary serenity in the company of certain people, but when you leave them, their warmth will quickly grow cold. Only the presence of the Lord gives you lasting and enduring serenity. The psalmist declared, "I will lift up mine eyes unto the hills, from whence cometh my help. My help cometh from the Lord" (Ps. 121:1). The help doesn't come from the hills but from the Lord.

I encourage you to take this lesson from Mary and develop serenity for the times of conflict and danger that are most certainly ahead. As a passionate kingdom woman on assignment by God, remember to relax and enjoy His presence every day, confident that regardless of what comes your way, He can handle it, He will bring you through it, and He will always make you victorious over it.

Serenity Is Found When Promise and Purpose Meet

Then took he him up in his arms, and blessed God, and said, Lord, now lettest thou thy servant depart in peace, according to thy word: For mine eyes have seen thy salvation.

Luke 2:28-30

A covenant was established between God and Simeon that he would not die until he saw the consolation of Israel, which was Jesus Christ. In Simeon's blessing we discover that this little baby Jesus had a purpose, which was to redeem humanity from sin and Satan's spiritual rule, beginning with the Jews first and then the Gentiles. When Jesus' purpose collided with Simeon's promise, serenity was established.

There are many women today who do not have kingdom passion in their lives because they do not understand their purpose, nor do they know what God has promised. It is so very important for you to know what God has promised because it is His promise that gives definition to your purpose and ultimately leads you to serenity.

You have a purpose beyond being a girlfriend, a housewife, a domestic engineer, a career woman, a mother, or a woman in the flower club at the church. Your purpose is beyond this. Your purpose as a kingdom woman is to institute serenity in whatever venue God has called you to: your home, your church, your job, your school, your neighborhood, and your community. When everyone else is in a rage, afraid, nervous, stressed out, and on the edge, you are the one appointed by God to walk in and speak serenity to that place and those people. How can you do this? You can do this because every day you are cultivating serenity, and the time you spend with the Lord gives you the certain faith and knowledge that nothing is too difficult for Him.

Knowing the Word of God and what God promises to you as a believer and His child will enable you to maintain your passion for the kingdom and define your purpose. And again, knowing the promise and finding your purpose brings eternal, lasting serenity into your life. When you bring that serenity into a chaotic and confusing situation, you diffuse all strategies of the enemy and establish the presence of God. Now that's the power of a kingdom woman who understands serenity!

Serenity Passes the Torch

> *And there was one Anna, a prophetess, the daughter of Phanuel, of the tribe of Aser: she was of a great age, and had lived with an husband seven years from her virginity;*
>
> *And she was a widow of about fourscore and four years, which departed not from the temple, but served God with fastings and prayers night and day.*
>
> *And she coming in that instant gave thanks likewise unto the Lord, and spake of him to all them that looked for redemption in Jerusalem.*
>
> Luke 2:36-38

A principle that we cannot neglect when it comes to serenity is that it often comes with time. Both Simeon and Anna are very old in years, and I don't believe the Holy Spirit writes anything to us without a good reason. While the age of Simeon is not mentioned, the fact that he says to the Lord, "now lettest thou thy servant depart in peace" (Luke 2:29), is a strong indication that he is an elderly figure who is not going to die until he sees the Messiah. The Scripture tells us that Anna was 84 and a widow, who lost her husband after seven years of marriage. Her passion was simply fasting and praying in the temple daily, waiting to see the Holy One of Israel. Both of these key figures have age and serenity.

I would like to encourage women who are in their sunset years. Maybe you are considering a retirement home or living in the fear of your children putting you in a nursing home. Maybe you believe that you can't compete with younger women anymore. You are too tired to go back to college, get another job, or even walk the malls to buy something nice to wear. If any of these scenarios describe your situation and you believe you have nothing to offer to God's kingdom at this time in your life, I beg to differ with you!

Look at Anna. She was widowed many, many years, and in Israel at that time, if you were a childless widow your were in the worst position you could be in. But Anna developed serenity that only living life for many years can develop, and that kind of serenity must be passed down to the younger women who are out on the front lines in spiritual battles. You will be amazed at the number of young ladies who are just waiting for you to whisper a word of encouragement in their ear about their menstrual cycle, caring for a husband, bearing children, and balancing life between the family and their ministry or work. You will be amazed at the number of young women who fear going through the change of life and look to you for advice and comfort.

You are needed now, as much as ever before, because when the preacher speaks to these young women, they often hear a voice of judgment or a standard that they don't know how to meet. When the doctor speaks, they often hear a voice that is concerned about their health but not necessarily their spirit. When the supervisor speaks they often hear a voice that is only interested in productivity and duty. When a friend speaks they often hear someone who is in competition or too self-absorbed to be compassionate. But when you speak—a woman of years, wisdom, and achievement—these young women hear a voice of experience, sensitivity, compassion, and understanding. You have nothing to gain by offering the benefit of your experience in life, and they can trust you. Trust is probably the most important ingredient in finding serenity. In trusting you, they learn to trust the God you have trusted all these years.

You do have a purpose; you do have a need to live because in a world of such chaotic conditions, there is nothing like having a voice who has survived wars, famines, depressions, and oppressions. We need someone to say, "If God brought us through before, God will bring us through again. If God made a way then, God can make a way now. So continue to trust God, and find peace and refuge in God's ability to provide exactly what you need for your life." Celebrate the serenity you have gained by passing it on to others who hunger for it. This is one of the most important kingdom assignments for a passionate kingdom woman.

17

THE STAMINA OF A KINGDOM WOMAN

Who can find a virtuous woman? for her price is far above rubies.

Proverbs 31:10

In the book of Proverbs, we find what today we would call, "the woman who has it all." Known as "the Proverbs 31 woman," she exemplifies and sets the standard for all kingdom women in the body of Christ.

- She is valued and praised by her husband (vv. 11,12, 23,28).

- She is praised and blessed by her children (v. 28).

- She rises before daybreak to cook for her children and feed her servants (v. 15).

- She manages and conducts businesses (vv. 16,18,24).

- She conditions her body and maintains physical strength (vv. 17,25).

- She opens her arms to the poor and the community (vv. 20,31).

- She secures provision for her family (vv. 13-14,19,21,27).

- She is dressed in the best clothing and her house is decorated with the best materials, much of which she makes herself (v. 22).

- She is wise and kind (v. 26).

Many daughters have done virtuously, but thou excellest them all.

Favour is deceitful, and beauty is vain: but a woman that feareth the Lord, she shall be praised.

Proverbs 31:29,30

What a woman! After reading through Proverbs 31, it is obvious to me that the most important thing a kingdom woman must have is stamina. The demands on her life cover many areas of endeavor and expertise, and she finds herself pulled by family, church, career, ministry, and other obligations and functions. It is interesting to me that in Proverbs 31, there are two verses that deal with physical strength.

She girdeth her loins with strength, and strengtheneth her arms.

Strength and honour are her clothing; and she shall rejoice in time to come.

Proverbs 31:17,25

While the emphasis on this woman's life has often been her sense of duty and all she was able to accomplish, I would like to consider that she had to do so much in so little time. When we consider all that this virtuous woman was able to achieve on a regular or daily basis, it is obvious to me that she had energy, vitality, fortitude, and the stamina to perform. If a kingdom woman is going to achieve all that God has for her life and maximize her potential for herself and those in her care, it is important that she develop stamina, which is the physical ability to go the distance.

Stamina Is Enhanced by Knowing the Role You Play and Doing It Gladly

We get the distinct impression from the Proverbs 31 woman that she was never confused as to what her role was. In the text, you never find her asking her husband, her servants, her children, or people in the marketplace what it is she is supposed to do. Obviously, she had discovered her gifts and callings long ago and had worked to develop them to the fullest. Then she just did everything she was called to do to the very best of her ability. She was clear on what she had to do and perhaps even why she was doing it. Knowing the role you are to play, the boundaries in which you are to work, is vital to maintaining stamina. There's nothing more stressful or a greater waste of energy than running around trying to figure out what you are supposed to be doing.

The Proverbs 31 woman goes one important step further, however. She did everything with wisdom and kindness (see verse 26). She knew that one of the secrets of maintaining stamina was to do all things with a heart of thanksgiving and gladness. Too many women waste energy complaining about and dreading what it is they know they have to do. Energy is expended making up excuses, putting off, and finding reasons not to perform the things that God has called them to perform. Whether it is caring for a loved one who is bedridden, raising a step-child, cleaning the church restroom, tackling a new territory to sell your product, or fixing dinner every night, if you take joy in these tasks, you will be much healthier and have more strength in the long run.

You cannot waste your energy debating over or regretting what God has called you to do in your home, your workplace, your church and ministry, or your social circles. Instead of using your energy to get out of responsibilities, use your energy to fulfill your kingdom assignments. It is easier to do this when you put them in proper perspective, which is knowing that God has given you those assignments. Out of all the people in the kingdom, He has entrusted you with those responsibilities and the people you are serving. And He will equip you and give you the stamina to see it through.

All of us are called to assignments that we may not enjoy or that we really didn't ask for, but when we begin to see that what we are doing is valued by God, that He has placed us in a position to carry out His will in the earth, it helps shed light on what would otherwise be a dark situation. Now your stamina is not developed for the situation, but your stamina is inspired because you are doing something for God, who chose you to do it. And where a heavy, resentful heart quenches stamina, a glad heart enhances and increases stamina.

It is important to know your role in the kingdom and set your heart to gladly fulfill that role. This is just another way of saying that you are fulfilling God's plan and desire for your life. Remember, the kingdom of God is His thoughts becoming our natural desires. Your stamina is increased when you understand that if God called you to play a certain role in the kingdom, He will give you the energy, fortitude, and strength to perform it. All the stamina you need is found in Him, so go for it!

Stamina Is Enhanced Through Order

This Proverbs 31 woman had to be extremely organized. She accomplished so much that she must have had a tremendous understanding of the importance of order. An organized kingdom woman orders her life. She sets priorities and plans ahead. Today there are too many women who lack organizational skills, don't know how to set priorities, and fail to order their lives. When they try to carry out their kingdom assignments without order, their energy goes in so many different directions at once that they burn out easily. Without order, stamina is difficult to develop and maintain.

I quickly discovered as a pastor that the people who feel like their lives are not flourishing or not going anywhere are those who lack order in their home, finances, professional life, lifestyle, and especially their spiritual lives. If your life is "out-of-order," then it is not working, is it? The enemy loves it when you do not have order in your life because it is easier for him to discourage you and stop you. Therefore, order is part of the fortress of wisdom and strength we are to build in our lives that keeps the enemy out.

Order reflects the excellence of God. He is not the author of confusion. Setting your life in order honors Him and gives Him glory while enabling you to be successful in all He's called you to do. Following are some helpful hints for establishing order in your life.

- Begin all tasks with prayer, asking God for His guidance.

- Write down your goals and objectives, giving realistic time frames.

- Create a nice filing system or get accustomed to using computer files to catalog information and make it easily accessible.

- Make a list of people who can help you accomplish your goals.

- Learn to delegate what you can delegate and establish a system to follow-up on the tasks you assign to others.

- Get comfortable with saying no. You are not superwoman. You cannot do it all.

- Purchase gadgets, luggage, or storage bins to organize home and travel.

- Keep a journal of your progress and celebrate your accomplishments.

Take the time today to plan tomorrow. Take time on Sunday evening to plan the following week. Take time on the last day of this month to plan the next month, and look at your year and the next few years periodically. Set your family's activities in order, organize your shopping, balance the time in your business with time having fun with friends, and work effectively and efficiently toward a successful future. Getting organized and setting your life in order enables you to channel your energy so that you can accomplish so much more. Establishing order in your life is key to maintaining stamina as a kingdom woman.

Stamina Is Enhanced Through Worship

My mother is a retired registered nurse. She did some amazing things when I was growing up. She worked the third shift as a nurse, was the wife to a pastor, was the mother to five children, and still found time to worship her Lord. This reminds me so much of the Proverbs 31 woman because I believe that she worshiped God wherever she was and in whatever she was doing. The Bible never mentions that the Proverbs 31 woman spent an hour in prayer, Bible study, and praise. But that doesn't mean that she wasn't doing it. I don't believe she could have maintained order, understood the role she was to play, or do all these things gladly if she didn't have a close relationship with God. It is impossible to have that much virtue, wisdom, favor, kindness—and stamina—without worshiping the Lord every day. Therefore, I conclude that her worship took place while she was doing her kingdom assignments.

Like my mother, who wore many hats of authority and responsibility at one time, kingdom women are often in demand and do not have the luxury of spending time alone with God for several hours a day. However, as a result they develop an incredible ability to see Him and know Him and praise Him at all times and in all situations. What a pleasure it is to worship God while you are accomplishing the tasks and the assignments He has called you to complete. Furthermore, a kingdom woman must learn that everything she says and does should be an act of worship to God.

It is possible for you to worship by helping your children with their homework, and while they are doing their arithmetic problems, you can be writing the passage of Scripture you're memorizing this month. You can worship God at a football or basketball game by supporting and encouraging your team. And between quarters and during the half-time, you can pull out your Bible and read the Word and be encouraged, or you can read this book and be enriched. Many women have discovered great times for reading at the Laundromat, in the airport, on the treadmill, or waiting for a bus. A kingdom woman will find time to worship, even if it means getting up earlier to have that special quiet time of prayer and meditation with God before her day begins.

Worship enables the kingdom woman to stay focused on God and what He's called her to be and do. Her batteries are recharged in worship. Her thinking is clarified in worship. Her priorities are set and her life is put in order in worship. And all of these elements increase and maintain her stamina. If you are unable to attend a place of worship or have a time apart from all other activities to worship, learn to worship right where you are.

The joy of the Lord is your strength.

Nehemiah 8:10

Worship brings joy to the heart, and joy endues our whole being with strength. My mother would worship while cooking a good meal. She would be stirring her soup with one hand and lifting the other to heaven, singing, "God, I adore You, I magnify You, I exalt you." I remember her driving down the highway, and every now and then I would look over and see a tear roll down her face while she listened to gospel music on the radio. I would see her read her Bible before church, so that when she got to church she had already entered into worship. What a legacy to leave a son!

Worship gives new perspective, vitality, and strength to make it through any situation or assignment that God is calling you to face, and all that adds up to stamina. When you have stamina, kingdom woman, you will run your race and win!

Man of God, woman of God, or child of God, I hope by now you have grasped the significance of what it means to have *Passion for Your Kingdom Purpose*. It is my sincere desire that this book has inspired you to ignite your passion for the kingdom and get busy with your assignment. I admonish you to not let fear, intimidation, denominational issues, negative people, or anything else hinder you from fulfilling God's call on your life.

Go forth as God has commanded you and walk intently with passion for your kingdom purpose. It is time for you to take the torch and run the race!

ENDNOTES

Chapter 1

[1] James Strong, LL.D., S.T.D., *The New Strong's Exhaustive Concordance of the Bible,* "Hebrew and Chaldee Dictionary," (Nashville, TN: Thomas Nelson Publishers, 1984), #6754.

[2] Spiros Zhodiates, *The Complete Word Study Dictionary-New Testament,* (Chattanooga, TN: AMG Publishers, 1993) p. 512.

[3] P. T. Forsyth, *A Sense of the Holy,* (Eugene, OR: Wipf & Stock Publishers, 1996), p. 73.

Chapter 2

[1] W. E. Vine, *Complete Expository Dictionary of Old And New Testament Words,* ed. Merrill F. Unger and William White (Nashville, TN: Thomas Nelson, Inc., 1985), p. 683.

[2] Spiros Zhodiates, *The Complete Word Study Dictionary-New Testament,* pp. 1262-1263.

Chapter 3

[1] P. T. Forsyth, *A Sense of the Holy,* pp. 97-98.

Chapter 4

[1] Donald W Musser and Joseph L. Price, *A New Handbook of Christian Theology* (Nashville, TN: Abingdon Press, 1992), p. 351.

[2] W. E. Vine, *Complete Expository Dictionary of Old And New Testament Words,* p. 307.

[3] Ibid., p. 307.

[4] Ibid., p. 478.

[5] Ibid., p. 412.

[6] http://search.netscape.com/ns/boomframe.jsp?query=Winifred+New man&page=1&offset=0&result_url=redir%3Fsrc%3Dwebsearch%2 6requestId%3D5aa148883a88c5ec%26clickedItemRank%3D9%26 userQuery%3DWinifred%2BNewman%26clickedItemURN%3Dhttp %253A%252F%252Fwww.geography.eku.edu%252FJONES%252F

planning.htm%26invocationType%3D-%26fromPage%3DAppleTop%26amp%3BampTest%3D1&remove_url=http%3A%2F%2Fwww.geography.eku.edu%2FJONES%2Fplanning.htm

Chapter 5

[1] Vernon McLellan, *Timeless Treasures: Classic Quotations for Speaking, Writing and Teaching* (Peabody, MA: Hendrickson Publishers, 1992), p. 201.

[2] W. E. Vine, *Complete Expository Dictionary of Old And New Testament Words*, p. 395.

[3] Carlyle Fielding Stewart III, *African American Church Growth: 12 Principles for Prophetic Ministry* (Nashville TN: Abingdon Press, 1994), p. 115.

Chapter 6

[1] Spiros Zhodiates, *The Complete Word Study Dictionary-New Testament*, p. 433.

[2] Ibid., pp. 375-377.

Chapter 7

[1] *Webster's New World College Dictionary*, Third Edition, Victoria Neufeldt, Editor-in-Chief (New York: Macmillan, Inc., 1996), p. 1107.

Chapter 8

[1] This quotation is taken from *The Millionaire Next Door*, by Thomas J. Stanley and William D. Danko (Marietta, GA: Longstreet Press, 1996).

[2] Bill Hull, *7 Steps To Transform Your Church* (Grand Rapids, MI: Fleming H. Revell of Baker Book House Company, 1993), p.124.

[3] W. E. Vine, *Complete Expository Dictionary of Old And New Testament Words*, p. 478.

[4] *Narcotics Anonymous*, 5th Edition (Chatsworth, CA: NA World Services, Inc., 1987), p. 17.

Chapter 10

[1] W. E. Vine, *Complete Expository Dictionary of Old And New Testament Words,* p.190.

[2] Spiros Zhodiates, *The Complete Word Study Dictionary-New Testament,* pp. 1244-1246.

[3] Roy B. Zuck, *The Speaker's Quote Book: Over 4500 Illustrations and Quotations for All Occasions* (Grand Rapids MI: Kregel Publications, 1997), p. 402.

[4] Ibid., p. 402.

Chapter 11

[1] *Webster's New World College Dictionary,* p. 391.

[2] W. E. Vine, *Complete Expository Dictionary of Old And New Testament Words,* p.678.

[3] Spiros Zhodiates, *The Complete Word Study Dictionary-New Testament,* p. 655.

[4] *Noah Webster's First Edition of An American Dictionary of the English Language* (San Franciso, CA: The Foundation for American Christian Education, 1983), "HER."

Chapter 12

[1] Spiros Zhodiates, *The Complete Word Study Dictionary-New Testament,* pp. 284-285.

[2] Quotations are taken from *Timeless Treasures: Classic Quotations for Speaking, Writing and Teaching,* by Vernon McLellan (Peabody, Massachusetts: Hendrickson Publishers, 1992).

Chapter 13

[1] W. E. Vine, *Complete Expository Dictionary of Old And New Testament Words,* p.545.

[2] Ibid., pp. 56-57.

Chapter 15

[1] Spiros Zhodiates, *The Complete Word Study Dictionary-New Testament,* pp. 805-806.

PRAYER OF SALVATION

God loves you—no matter who you are, no matter what your past. God loves you so much that He gave His one and only begotten Son for you. The Bible tells us that "...whoever believes in him shall not perish but have eternal life" (John 3:16 NIV). Jesus laid down His life and rose again so that we could spend eternity with Him in heaven and experience His absolute best on earth. If you would like to receive Jesus into your life, say the following prayer out loud and mean it from your heart.

> *Heavenly Father, I come to You admitting that I am a sinner. Right now, I choose to turn away from sin, and I ask You to cleanse me of all unrighteousness. I believe that Your Son, Jesus, died on the cross to take away my sins. I also believe that He rose again from the dead so that I might be forgiven of my sins and made righteous through faith in Him. I call upon the name of Jesus Christ to be the Savior and Lord of my life. Jesus, I choose to follow You and ask that You fill me with the power of the Holy Spirit. I declare that right now I am a child of God. I am free from sin and full of the righteousness of God. I am saved in Jesus' name. Amen.*

If you prayed this prayer to receive Jesus Christ as your Savior for the first time, please contact us on the Web at **www.harrisonhouse.com** to receive a free book.

Or you may write to us at:

Harrison House

P.O. Box 35035

Tulsa, Oklahoma 74153

ABOUT THE AUTHOR

Dr. Sir Walter L. Mack Jr. is noted for his national and international ministry, stemming from community-focused work. As pastor and teacher of the 2,800-member Union Baptist Church in Winston-Salem, NC, Dr. Mack is dedicated to the cause of Jesus Christ, and he continues to have a profound impact for the kingdom of God as he inspires and motivates others to operate in a spirit of excellence while using their gifts and talents for God.

Continuing study at Oxford and Harvard University, Dr. Mack earned a Bachelor of Arts degree in Mass Communications from Elon College in Elon, North Carolina, a Master of Divinity degree from Duke University in Durham, North Carolina, and a Doctor of Ministry degree from United Theological Seminary in Dayton, Ohio. He is devoted to the promotion of education and dedicated to continual advancement.

Dr. Mack is a strong proponent of ministry beyond the four walls of the church. His global work began with missions trips to Haiti and Israel, and he has ministered on three continents. His work is perpetuated nationally as leaders, pastors, conference organizers, and political officials request his passionate preaching, ardent teaching, and zealous training for the enlightenment of their followers, as well as duplication of the programs he has created and implemented.

Dr. Mack is a gospel jazz enthusiast who enjoys family gatherings and gut-wrenching humor as he pursues the passion of his kingdom purpose.

To contact Dr. Sir Walter L. Mack Jr.
please write:

Dr. Sir Walter L. Mack Jr.
P. O. Box 1919
Clemmons, NC 27012

*Please include your prayer requests
and comments when you write.*

Fast. Easy.
Convenient.

For the latest Harrison House product information and author news, look no further than your computer. All the details on our powerful, life-changing products are just a click away. New releases, E-mail subscriptions, Podcasts, testimonies, monthly specials—find it all in one place. Visit harrisonhouse.com today!

harrisonhouse